'Stock Investing Game Plan Sell After Earnings Report'
A Stock Trading Method

INTRODUCTION

The book 'Stock Investing Game Pan Sell After Earnings Report' A stock trading method is written for a non-financial person, financial professional, non-experienced retail stock trader or experienced stock trader. Your qualified stock for your Stock Investing Game Plan Sell After Earnings Report a stock trading method are based on your stock research (free on the internet) and selection process with a proven time to purchase a stock methodology of 3 to 4 trading days or more before a stock earnings release date and when to give your broker your stock to sell at a profit. With the Stock Investing Game Plan Sell After Earnings Report a stock trading method Spread Sheet on your computer program, allows you with a recent stock market price to visualize your potential stock trade flat dollar ($) or percent (%) profit before you give your stock trade to your broker. It is written to help the average American hourly or salary worker, retired person, home owner or renter with $25,000 or large money sum to become financial independent, add to their retirement income, their own boss, make money, increase their wealth and live the comfortable life that they always wanted or dreamed.

The stock market does provide a person or family both the opportunity to make money, be their own boss, make money, increase their wealth and live comfortable. But like all things in life, there is risk of loss or all of your investment and requires you to complete research work and to set your stock trading goals. With the Stock Investing Game Plan Sell After Earnings Report a stock trading method you have the opportunity to maximize your returns. This investment strategy allows a person or family to earn money while other people are just getting by. Some people do not invest, use a buy and hold investment strategy that s controlled by the investor or broker or invest randomly selected stocks. When compared to the Stock Investing Game Plan Sell After Earnings Report a stock trading method, the other investment strategies do not have you in control of your means and to maximize your wealth creation.

If you are concerned about mastering the Stock Investing Game Plan Sell After Earnings Report a stock trading method and to maximize your returns, then you should paper trade stocks that allow you to navigate stock potential purchase and sell transactions and to obtain experience and confidence to move into actual money stock trading with your stock broker. The book is published to develop your Stock Investing Game Plan Sell After Earnings Report a stock trading method skills, experience and history that allows you and your family to become your own boss, make money, create wealth and live the comfortable that you have always wanted and dreamed.

A Stock Investing Game Plan Sell After Earnings Report a stock trading method features and advantages are

- With your on-line computer or cell phone app you can complete stock trade transactions at home or anywhere
- Minimum Stock Investing Game Plan Sell After Earnings Report a stock trading method training that can be accomplished with paper trading
- With the Stock Investing Game Plan Sell After Earnings Report a stock trading method on your computer program, the Spread Sheet allows you with a recent stock market price to visualize your potential stock trade flat dollar ($) or (%) percent profit before you give your stock trade to your broker
- No additional investment programs required
- No stock analysis experience required but willingness to complete stock research
- Become financial independent
- Add to your retirement income
- Be your own boss
- Make money ($) & enjoy life
- Increase your wealth
- You & your family live comfortable
- Grow you money ($) sum
- Easy to acquire Stock Investing Game Plan Sell After Earnings Report a stock trading method skills
- If power goes down at your house and with a cell phone app and paper printed Stock Investing Game Plan Sell After Earnings Report a stock trading method Work Sheets and Computer Spread Sheet you complete stock trades
- Spend your free or idle time making ($) instead of playing games

- Teach your family members or friends or create a Stock Investing Game Plan Sell After Earnings Report a stock trading method club.

What Is Stock Investing Game Plan Sell After Earnings Report A Stock Trading Method

The Stock Investing Game Plan Sell After Earnings Report A Stock Trading Method has three steps. First use Initial and Final Note Pads to complete stock research (free on the internet) from financial companies. On a Final Note Pad to qualify stocks that are best for Stock Investing Game Plan Sell After Earnings Report A Stock Trading Method. Second step transfer qualified stock information on a computer Work Sheet and Spread Sheet. 3 to 5 days prior to a qualified stock earnings release date have a broker complete a stock purchase transaction. Enter a stock break-even purchase price in the Work Sheet and Spread Sheet. Last step entered stock market prices onto the computer Spread Sheet that calculates a potential stock profit above a stock break-even purchase price. When the stock profit price matches an investor's investment goal, sell a stock through a broker.

How To Use Stock Investing Game Plan Sell After Earnings Report A Stock Trading Method

A Stock Investing Game Plan Sell After Earnings Report A Sock Trading Method basically has three simple and easy steps.   First step complete stock research (free on the internet) from financial companies onto Initial and Final Note Pads. On a Final Note Pad has qualified stocks for a Stock Investing Game Plan Sell After Earnings Report A Stock Trading Method investment.   Second step transfer the qualified stocks by earnings release per month, day and detailed stock information onto a computer Work Sheet and Spread Sheet. Completes a qualified stock purchase through a stock broker and enter stock break-even purchase price onto a Work Sheet and Spread Sheet.   Third step enter stock market prices onto a computer Spread Sheet that calculates a stock potential profit. When a stock profit is above a stock purchase price that matches an investment goal have a broker sell a stock and enter price into the computer.

How Much To Use Initial In Stock Investing Game Plan Sell After Earnings Report A Stock Trading Method

A Stock Investing Game Plan Sell After Earnings Report A Stock Trading Method allows a person with available money to invest in the stock market. The available money is not required to meet your family living expenses. A Stock Investing Game Plan Sell After Earnings Report A Stock Trading Method can work with $25,000 as a minimum to start. The money allows the 200 to 300 shares purchase 1 to 3 medium priced stocks.   With a larger money sum, there is greater flexibility to purchase a large stock number or stocks from different corporations.   If a Stock Investing Game Plan Sell After Earnings Report A Stock Trading Method has profits invested into additional qualified stocks. The end of year profit results are similar to compounding interest to build a greater sum to invest.

Who Should Use Stock Investing Game Plan Sell After Earnings Report A Stock Trading Method

A Stock Investing Game Plan Sell After Earnings Report A Stock Trading Method is used by a person with available funds ($25,000 or more dollars) to invest in the stock market. A person must have sufficient free time to complete stock research and a stock broker. A person with no stock market experience can master a Stock Investing Game Plan Sell After Earnings Report A Stock Trading Method procedure by reading the book and paper trading on a computer. A Stock investing Game Plan Sell After Earnings Report A Stock Trading Method investors are people who (1) are retired and desire additional income and to keep their mind sharp, (2) enjoy winning in a game, (3) seek to increase their wealth and cash inflow, (4) desire quick and easy access to their money not like real estate or an annuity, (5) want an easy and quick simple investment strategy, (6) want to organize an investment club with a stock investment strategy, (7) want to be their own boss, (8) desire to compound their profits, (9) want to live a comfortable life with what they have always wanted and dreamed and (10) want an additional checking account, access to a loan or purchase stocks on margin.

When To Use Stock Investing Game Plan Sell After Earnings ReportA Stock Trading Method

A Stock Investing Game Plan Sell After Earnings Report A Stock Trading Method is used to earn profits from trading stocks. The trading method is very flexible, simple and easy to use in all stock market movements except it is difficult in a bear market or during economic/political problem times. Best stock market conditions are (1) in regular trading sessions with good economic/political times, (2) stock earnings seasons, (3) in a progressive industry sector with stock that have a upward price movement, (4) in a bull market and (5) invest in growth stocks with good/increasing quarterly sales, good earnings per share and good management guidance.

Why Use Stock Investing Game Plan Sell After Earnings Report A Stock Trading Method
A Stock Investing Game Plan Sell After Earnings Report A Stock Trading Method is a simple and easy stock investment strategy. After you have a stock broker and with paper trading you have mastered a Stock Investing Game Plan Sell After Earnings Report A Stock Trading Method three steps, you are ready to use cash with a Stock Investing Game Plan Sell After Earnings Report A Stock Trading Method. You complete your stock research (free on the internet) that determines qualified stocks and you have a broker complete a stock market purchase. After a future stock price matches your investment goal, then a broker sells a stock.

   With a Stock Investing Game Plan Sell After Earnings Report A Stock Trading Method you can establish a stock trading club with your friends, teach your family to trade stocks, increase your wealth, cash inflow and economic independence and access your money very quick.

CHAPTER 1

WHY INVEST WITH STOCK INVESTING GAME PLAN SELL AFTER EARNINGS REPORT A STOCK TRADING METHOD

Why Use Stock Investing Game Plan Sell After Earnings Report A Stock Trading Method

The Stock Investing Game Plan Sell After Earnings Report a stock trading method directs you (retail stock investor) to complete your own stock research (free on the internet) and on-line qualified stock purchase and sell transactions through your stock broker account to be your own boss, make money, increase wealth or to live comfortable. For each earnings release month and earnings release day of a month with Before Market (BM), During Market (DH) or After Market (AF) abbreviations earnings release time of trading day, earnings release alpha character day of a week and analyst earnings estimates you determine qualified stocks to trade with the Stock Investing Game Plan Sell After Earnings Report a stock trading method for a profit. Within most months of a year, there are a large number of qualified stocks. These stocks earnings releases are repeated every 3 months of a year. This means with some stock research to confirm a stock ranking that there is a great potential for your present (one month) Stock Investing Game Plan Sell After Earnings Report a stock trading method winners turning them into repeat winners.

Another similar stock investing approach is a momentum investing approach that has you (an investor) purchase a stock at a high market price and sell your stock at a higher stock market price. Stock Investing Game Plan Sell After Earnings Report a stock trading method is similar to momentum investing but there are differences. The differences are (1) you do not have to develop stock trends to identify qualified stocks, (2) you base stocks for Stock Investing Game Plan Sell After Earnings Report a stock trading method on stocks that you have researched (free on the internet) and determined to be qualified stocks and (3) after earnings release to sell a stock through your borker.

What Are The Major Requirements To Use The Stock Investing Game Plan Sell After Earnings Report A Stock Trading Method

To consider the Stock Investing Game Plan Sell After Earnings Report a stock trading method your requirements are several, These major requirements are (1) time to qualify your considered stock symbols, (2) have $25,000 or more dollars for your investment, (3) have a computer and printer, (4) know each qualified stock earnings release important dates, (5) know your broker stock purchase cost and most recent stock market prices, (6) establish your stock trading profit goals and (7) when you have a profit have your broker sell your stock.

When Or Time To Qualify Your Considered Stock Investing Game Plan Sell After Earnings Report A Stock Trading Method Stock Symbols

Time to qualify your considered stock symbols is time that you required to complete your stock research and is usually 3 to 4 days prior to a stock earnings release date . The stock research (free on the internet) assures that your selected stocks have minimal risk of loss or good expected earnings release. The author qualified stock standard was using two financial company stock earnings release rankings. These companies rankings are Zack's digital racking of 1 (strong buy) and 2 (buy) combined and GOOGL/NASDAQ/Zacks colored in the green middle ranking that got 2 stars (buy).

How Many Dollars ($25,000 Or More Dollars) For Your Stock Investing Game Plan Sell After Earnings Report A Stock Trading Method Investment

The next major Stock Investing Game Plan Sell After Earnings Report a stock trading method consideration is your investment money. To invest with the Stock Investing Game Plan Sell After Earnings Report a stock trading method you have a minimum of $25,000 or more money. The minimum $25,000 sum allows you with an opportunity start trading with Stock Investing Game Plan Sell After Earnings Report a stock trading method and to purchase 200 or 300 shares between two companies. If the stock market price is a low price, then a company stock quantity could greater. With your trading profits, you will be able to purchase additional company shares or a greater share number for one company. It is true with a larger investment money sum you have the opportunity to purchase a greater number of company shares or multiple company shares which are determined by a stock market price.

What Equipment You Required Is A Computer & Printer

To have an efficient and effective Stock Investing Game Plan Sell After Earnings Report a stock trading method you require a computer (on-line to your broker) and printer. With a computer you are able to program the computer with a Stock Investing Game Plan Sell After Earnings Report a stock trading method Work Sheet & stock Spread Sheet.

After you enter your earnings release month/day qualified stocks in the proper format with (1) earnings release month first stock and the other stock information and (2) your broker stock purchase transaction price with added allowance for commissions and exchange fees.

After these entries and a recent stock market price, your computer can project your potential profit on your stock Spread Sheet. The projected profit allows you to compare the profit to your investment goals that determines your desire to sell. After the broker complete a stock sell transaction and you enter the price into the computer, it calculates your trading performance on your stock Work Sheet and Spread Sheet. Your Spread Sheet becomes your trading performance record for future stock research.

Stock Investing Game Plan Sell After Earnings Report A Stock Trading Method Compared To Casino Or Lottery Gambling

Many friends and people have referred to stock market investing with any strategy is just like gambling at a casino or playing the lottery. This statement is partially true due to both activities have the potential of your money loss or to win to increase your wealth. This potential money loss or wealth gain are possibilities same as investing the stock market. But Stock Investing Game Plan Sell After Earnings Report A Stock Trading Method or other stock investment strategy is not similar to gambling in the Casino or playing the Lottery due to several reasons. These are (1) with stock market investing you are investing in a corporation (a business) and you have the right to receive a stock certificate of corporate ownership, (2) you complete your stock research to identify qualified stocks, 3 to 4 days before earnings release purchase a through your stock broker and (3) after earnings release sell a stock through a broker.

In Stock Earnings Season Use Stock Investing Game Plan Sell After Earnings Report A Stock Trading Method
A stock investor can use Stock Investing Game Plan Sell After Earnings Report a stock trading method as an excellent trading strategy for stock earnings season (very high number of companies report earnings within a few months) or for any time during the year (stock regular earnings season). Since the Stock Investing Game Plan Sell After Earnings Report a stock trading method requires an investor to complete stock research to qualify stocks, during stock earnings season and investor will complete stock research. When stock earnings season is compared to the regular stock earning season, the stock earnings season has a greater number of stock researches to qualify stocks. This fact means that an investor will spend additional stock research time (free on the internet) to be prepared for investing in stock earnings season qualified stocks.

Where To Find Stock Investing Game Plan Sell After Earnings Report A Stock Trading Method Report Date & Information
After an investor learns of a company (symbol) with a good potential for an excellent earnings report, then an investor has to obtain a company's projected earnings date information. A company (symbol) earnings date information is obtain (free on the internet) from one of the following financial company reports. These are (1) Zack's Earnings Calendar, Earnings Report or Stock Overview & Earnings page, (2) From browser or GOOGL Chrome GOOGL/Zacks/NASDAQ, (3) Yahoo Earnings Calendar, Company Quote Page and Financial news, (4) broker such as Schwab Company Research Page, (5) Bloomberg Calendar of Earnings and (6) use your past Work Sheets.

Know Each Qualified Stock Investing Game Plan Sell After Earnings Report A Stock Trading Method Information
With the Stock Investing Game Plan Sell After Earnings Report a stock trading method it is a must for you to know each qualified stock earnings release information. A stock's earnings release information is a major factor that determines a stock earnings

release day of a month and earnings release trading day time to sell a stock. A Stock Investing Game Plan Sell After Earnings Report a stock trading method earnings release information (free on the internet) includes (1) digital notation for earnings release month, (2) digital notation for earnings release day of a month, (3) alpha character earnings notation for release time of a trading day and (4) alpha character earnings release day of week. For each qualified stock, this earning release stock information is entered into your computer Work Sheet & Spread Sheet. The stock entry sequence has a stock with first day of the month with a before market open notation, next during market regular hours and after market hours notation. Next in the sequence are the second Stock Investing Game Plan Sell After Earnings Report a stock trading method day of a month stocks. The sequence is repeated until the last Stock Investing Game Plan Sell After Earnings Report a stock trading method day of a month.

With this earning release stock sequence by earnings release day of month and trading day time on the Work Sheet & Spread Sheet, you are aware and can anticipate when each qualified stock within a month is ready to have earnings release. This helps you complete a timely purchase and anticipate the day and time of trading to sell.

Know Your Stock Purchase Break-Even Cost
The next major Stock Investing Game Plan Sell After Earnings Report a stock trading method major factor is you must know your broker stock purchase cost and break-even costs. A stock break-even cost consists of your brokers purchase price plus added cost for a broker's purchase and sell commissions plus exchange fee. Your stock break-even purchase cost is the major trading costs along with your stock broker sell price that determines your stock trading profit.

Establish Your Investment Profit Goal
Your investment profit goal us an important consideration due to it sets the profit standard for your trading activity. Your investment goal options are (1) flat ($) profit or return or (2) percent (%) return on invested dollars. In your computer (1) you enter your stock purchase break-even price, (2) as you obtain a stock recent trading price you enter it into the computer to calculate your

potential profit and (3) after stock broker stock sell price, you enter it into your computer to provide your actual profit.

Have Your Broker Sell Stock
Your final consideration after a market stock price profit projection is to pull the sell trigger by giving your broker your stock to sell. Since Stock Investing Game Plan Sell After Earnings Report a stock trading method has you through your broker to sell a stock on earnings release day and you have a sizeable profit in a high quality stock, it is difficult to complete a broker sell transaction.

Record Your Stock Investing Game Plan Sell After Earnings Report A Stock Trading Method Report Work Sheets To Build Your Future Qualified Stock List
Your past month completed Stock Investing Game Plan Sell After Earnings Report a stock trading method Work Sheets (identified with each past earnings release month and stock purchase day) are your stock trading performance records. These are considered another stock qualifying factor. On your past month Work Sheet each stock has a broker purchase and sell trade transaction prices and each stock trading performance as stated in $ profit or $ loss or % return on investment. Since all corporations are required to issue earnings releases every 3 months, your stock completed Work Sheet shows how well each stock performed for a past earnings release day of a month. With some slight variances due to calendar days and corporation selected earnings release date, every 3 groups of stock month earnings releases can be grouped into month groups. These groups are Group 1 months (January, April, July & October), Group 2 months (February, May, August & November) and Group 3 months (March, April, September & December) (See Exhibit 1 – 1).

After establishing a few months of complete stock Work Sheets, you can conduct your stock research to develop your qualified stock list. The stock list would have each stock's flat ($) dollar gains and % percent return on invested funds. This feature means that your stock list has stocks with a good probability as winners for the next month earnings release session.

With a high number of qualified stocks with good past earnings release performance, you complete most of your stock trade transactions for a profit. Your stock trade transaction profit options allow you to invest your money and or complete as many qualified stock trade transactions as

EXHIBIT 1 – 1

STOCK INVESTING GAME PLAN SELL AFTER EARNINGS REPORT TRADING METHOD ANTICIPATING COMMON STOCK TO REPEAT EARNINGS BY MONTH GROUPING

GROUP 1	GROUP 2	GROUP 3
JANUARY (1)	FEBRUARY (2)	MARCH (3)
APRIL (4)	MAY (5)	JUNE (6)
JULY (7)	AUGUST (8)	SEPTEMBER (9)
OCTOBER (10)	NOVEMBER (11)	DECEMER (12)

possible. This investment approach allows you to build your investment wealth by basically compounding your earnings release stock profits into additional earnings release stock trade transactions and profits. With this concept within a month group, you take your initial earnings release stock profits and purchase additional qualified stocks for your next earnings release stock investment. With your earnings release per share standard quantity stock investment profits, you continue to invest in qualified stocks with same stock share quantity. If there are individual qualified stocks, the concept allows you to invest in a company with a smaller stock share quantity such as high market priced stocks (less than your standard share quantity). By investing in additional qualified earnings release stocks, you have an opportunity to increase your wealth. The wealth increase opportunity is similar to compound interest on a quarter or month bases to have a high annual yield or to take your earnings release stock profits and build your cash stock broker account and wait for a stock in the next month that it is expected to
report earnings.

A Stock Investing Game Plan Sell After Earnings Report a stock trading method recap results of example of re-investing stock investment money and earnings release stock profits into additional qualified stocks are shown in (Exhibit 1 – 2). A recap for a 3 month period and from a $25,000 initial investment, a net flat dollar return (less trade commission & exchange fees) of $46,499 or a 86% percent return on invested money ($).

With the Stock Investing Game Plan Sell After Earnings Report a stock trading method there is a great opportunity for an individual to purchase and sell stock for a profit. You (an investor) can combine your stock profits with your investment money to purchase and sell additional stocks to compound your profits. An outline of a Stock Investing Game Plan Sell After Earnings Report a stock trading method events show how simple and easy it is to complete stock purchases and sales through your broker and earn a profit. (See Exhibit 1 – 3).

A Stock Investing Game Plan Sell After Earnings Report a stock trading method as outline in the future chapters provides you with the insights, ability and desire to use Stock Investing Game Plan Sell After Earnings Report a stock trading method as you stock investment strategy.   With a Stock Investing Game Plan Sell After Earnings Report a stock trading method you devote some work to stock research (free on the internet), completing purchase and sell trade transactions through your stock broker account, record keeping. You can teach your family to help and participate. But you have an opportunity to make a lot of Dollars. Give-up computer game playing, watching TV or loafing on a couch and with a Stock Investing Game Plan Sell After Earnings Report a stock trading method become your own boss and make money, increase your wealth and live comfortable.

Use Of Industry Sector For Stock Investing Game Plan Sell After Earnings Report A Stock Trading Method
You as an investor desire to start industry sector investing, then you have multiple steps to identify qualified stocks for your Stock Investing Game Plan Sell After Earnings Report a

EXHIBIT 1 - 2

STOCK INVESTING GAME PLAN SELL AFTER EARNINGS REPORT
A STOCK TRADING METHOD INVESTOR RESULTS RECAP

WITH $25,000 INVESTMENT MONEY

MONTH 1		MONTH 2		MONTH 3		MONTH 4	
WEEK	PROFIT	WEEK	PROFIT	WEEK	PROFIT	WEEK	PROFIT
1	1,563	1	2,177	1	2,581	1	3,034
2	1,689	2	901	2	1,264	2	3,333
3	1,390	3	2,448	3	2,719	3	2,969
4	2,590	4	3,478	4	4,818	4	3,569
5	1,525	5	2,240	5	3,071	0	0
TOTAL	8,757		11,244		14,453		12,905
LESS (*)	-140		-200		-240		-280
NET ($)	8,617		11,044		14,213		12,625

NET FLAT DOLLAR RETURN $46,499-$25,000= $21,499
% RETURN ON $25,000 $21,499/$25,000 = 86%
TRADE COMMISIONS AND EXCHANGE FEES AT $10 PER TRADE

stock trading method. Industry sector investing has an investor purchase businesses or corporations stocks that have their sales obtained from the same product or service. A term to describe the industry sector profit results is an incoming tide lifts all boats. Many financial companies provide industry sector lists that cover the USA economy.

A list that best fits a Stock Investing Game Plan Sell After Earnings Report a stock trading method investor's objective is difficult to find. Some industry sector lists subtitles are presented in Exhibit (1 - 4).

The author's approach to industry sector investing research for potential Stock Investing Game Plan Sell After Earnings Report a stock trading method stocks is a simple multiple step process. These steps require a pen/paper, computer and some investor research time (free on the internet).   All the information is located on the internet and is free. The stock industry sector research is basically separating the wheat from chaft or with an industry sector list to identifying qualified stocks for your Stock Investing Game Plan Sell After Earnings Report a stock trading method investment.

The author's industry sector investing research and Stock Investing Game Plan Sell After Earnings Report a stock trading method approach has several steps. These steps are (1) identify your selected industry sector, (2) on your computer access the internet or GOOGL chrome for research, (3) with pen and paper as first entry list the stocks onto a stock Initial Note Pad and Final Note Pad, (4) qualify your Final Note Pad stock list, (5) by earnings release day of month identified and separate qualified stocks, (6) from your stock Final Note Pad transfer by earnings release day of a month with abbreviation for earnings release time of trading day to your stock Work Sheet and Computer Spread Sheet and (7) for your record keeping and future reference (a) properly identify industry sector your stock Final Note Pad. This could include your stock performance and (b) you properly update your stock Work Sheet with your broker stock purchase and sell transaction prices.

The first step to identify your industry sector for potential Stock Investing Game Plan Sell After Earnings Report a stock trading method investment is for you to identify your industry sector of interest. From reading printed, internet and TV news, you become aware of an industry sector that has been mentioned to have anticipated impressive growth. If an industry sector has expected growth, then it means at least several (leaders) companies within the sector are expected to make major contributions to the growth. If you are able to identify these companies that will make the major contribution to the sector sales growth, then you have potential stocks for your Stock Investing Game Plan Sell After Earnings Report a stock trading method investment that will make a stock trading profit.

The second step is to review your past stock Final Note Pads and Work Sheets with an industry sector that will show stocks past performance,

The third step is to access your computer internet or GOOGL/NASDAQ/ZACKs to search for industry sector stock by entering a request. Examples are defense stock list, travel stock list, chip stock list, semi-conductor stock list, broad cast radio & TV and internet commerce stock list.

Both step two and three provide a random list of corporate names or stock symbols.

EXHIBIT 1 – 3

STOCK INVESTING GAME PLAN SELL ATER EARNINGS REPORT A STOCK TRADING METHOD STOCK PURCHASE AND SELL EVENTS

SIGPSAER = STOCK INVESTING GAME PLAN SELL AFTER EARNINGS REPORT

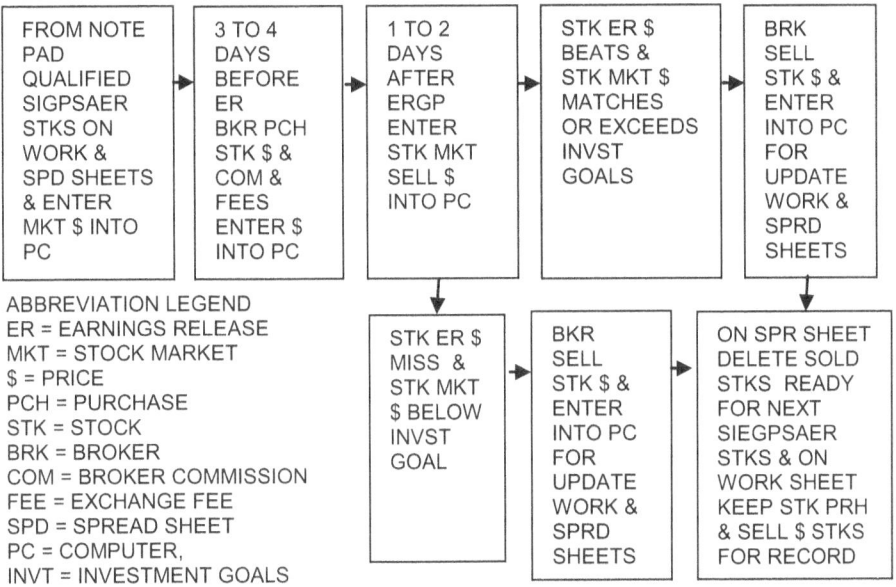

| FROM NOTE PAD QUALIFIED SIGPSAER STKS ON WORK & SPD SHEETS & ENTER MKT $ INTO PC | 3 TO 4 DAYS BEFORE ER BKR PCH STK $ & COM & FEES ENTER $ INTO PC | 1 TO 2 DAYS AFTER ERGP ENTER STK MKT SELL $ INTO PC | STK ER $ BEATS & STK MKT $ MATCHES OR EXCEEDS INVST GOALS | BRK SELL STK $ & ENTER INTO PC FOR UPDATE WORK & SPRD SHEETS |

ABBREVIATION LEGEND
ER = EARNINGS RELEASE
MKT = STOCK MARKET
$ = PRICE
PCH = PURCHASE
STK = STOCK
BRK = BROKER
COM = BROKER COMMISSION
FEE = EXCHANGE FEE
SPD = SPREAD SHEET
PC = COMPUTER,
INVT = INVESTMENT GOALS

| STK ER $ MISS & STK MKT $ BELOW INVST GOAL | BKR SELL STK $ & ENTER INTO PC FOR UPDATE WORK & SPRD SHEETS | ON SPR SHEET DELETE SOLD STKS READY FOR NEXT SIEGPSAER STKS & ON WORK SHEET KEEP STK PRH & SELL $ STKS FOR RECORD |

Your next step is to qualify and industry rank your industry sector potential stocks on your Final Note Pad. For this step you refer to one or several of your stock research company's earnings report (free on the internet). Some of these research companies are Zacks, Yahoo, GOOGL/NASDAQ/ZACKs and Bloomberg.

First phase is to qualify each stock with all the important Stock Investing Game Plan Sell After Earnings Report a stock trading method information. This stock information includes (a) earnings release month, (b) earnings release day of a month, (c) earnings release time of trading day as alpha character notation, (d) 2 analyst earnings ranking, (e) from a calendar earnings release day of week alpha notation and (f) each stock symbol.

The second phase of this step is to ranking each stock within the industry sector. To identify the major company (stock) contributors to an industry sector growth you can use Zacks earning report. The earnings report identifies each stock industry ranking such as top 17% (43 out of 256) and sector ranking top 16% (1 out of 6). (See Exhibit 1 – 4)

After you complete qualifying of your stocks and you identify your industry sector stocks for Stock Investing Game Plan Sell After Earnings Report a stock trading method, your next step is transfer all the stock pertinent trading information from your stock Final Note Pad onto your stock Work Sheet and Computer Spread Sheet.

You are ready to start trading your selected stocks for an industry sector. After you enter your broker stock purchase break-even stock price onto your computer spread sheet, then when your broker sells your stock you enter the sell transaction price into your computer program. Your computer program calculates your trading performance.

Your final step is to assure your stock Work Sheet has the broker purchase and sell stock prices and calculated your stock trading performance. Also, you assure that your stock Work Sheet is identified with the industry sector name.

Actual Stock Investing Game Plan Sell After Earnings Report A Stock Trading Method 3 Month Results

The strategy results have increased my opportunity to make a lot of DOLLARS (Benjamin's). My Stock Investing Game Plan Sell After Earnings Report a stock trading method started January 1, 2019 through April 30, 2019. As of February 31, 2019, my Stock Investing Game Plan Sell After Earnings Report a stock trading method profits were before margin interest (borrowing stock) and without margin interest would have been.

EXHIBIT 1 - 4

INDUSTRY SECTOR STOCK (BUSINESS OR CORPORATE) LIST

Aerospace,
Agriculture,
Alcohol/Tobacco,
Apparel clothing and shoes,
Automotive /trucks/parts ,
Banks,
Building construction,
 Business/service,
Chemical,
Chip manufactures and equipment,
Computer,
Consumer,
Electronics/products/science/measure,
Energy/oil & gas/ coal/drill & explore/re-newable/transport,
Finance & loans,
Food & beverage & meat/dairy/grain,
Insurance life & accident & health,
 Internet network & connection,
Leisure/lodging/service/home/travel,
Machine production,
Media, print & Radio & TV,
Medical, drugs//service/products/out-patient/ systems & equipment/ supplies/managed care/hospital,
Metal Fabrication/ Steel producing, steel specialty
Mines gold, silver and gems
Miscellaneous
Real Estate development
Retail Mail order/mini-markets/home furnishing/restaurants/drug store/jewelry/discount/department
    store/electronics/auto &parts/office supplies/leisure
Savings & Loan
Software Soft & design/security/medical/data base/entertainment/gaming
Telecom wireless/infrastructure/cable & satellite/fiber optics
Transport Rail/trucks/ship/air/air freight/ logistics equipment
Utility electric power/gas/water supply

EXHIBIT 1 – 5

STOCK INVESTING GAME PLAN SELL AFTER EARNINGS REPORT
TRADING METHOD A STOCK TRADING PERFORMANCE

Month	Margin Interest	Month With Interest	YTD W/Margin Interest	No Margin MTD	No Margin YTD
Jan	$2,209	$29.543	$29,543	$31,752	$31,752
Feb	$3,673	$53,304	$82,847	$56,668	$88,419
Mar	$2,794	$8,527	$91,374	$11,907	$100,326

CHAPTER 2

OPEN A STOCK BROKER ACCOUNT

Steps To Determined Your Stock Broker & Account Types
For you (investor) to complete a stock purchase and sell trade
transaction, it has to be completed through an individual broker or
broker associated with a large stock broker corporation.   To
complete your stock trade transactions, first you must open a
stock broker account with an individual broker or large stock
broker firm. You can find broker firms on the internet, from a
friend, newspapers, magazines or TV. There are many steps that
you as a potential stock investor must complete to open stock
broker account.   (See Exhibit 2 – 1)

EXHIBIT 2 – 1

OBTAIN A STOCK BROKER FLOW CHART

DESIRE TO INVEST IN THE STOCK MARKET

YOUR STOCK MARKET GOALS OR OBJECTIVES FLAT DOLLAR $ INCREASE OR % PERCENT RETURN ON INVESTED $

OBTAIN STOCK BROKER LIST & INTERVIEW STOCK BROKERS ACCOUNT TYPE   CASH OR MARGIN MINIMUM DOLLARS ($) AMOUNT CASH QUANTITY TO OPEN & TO MAINTAIN ON-LINE COMPUTER TRADING CELL PHONE TRADING APP EXTENDED HOURS TRADING TRANSACTION FEES ($) & EXCHANGE FEES ($) WHO CONTROLS THE ACCOUNT INDIVIDUALOR BROKER & COSTS AVAILABE TRAINING PROGRAM OR PAPER TRADING AVAILALBE EDUCATIONAL PROGRAMS & SEMINARS AVAILALBE CHECKING, LOAN & OTHER FINANCIAL FEATURES

SELECT & OPEN STOCK BROKER ACCOUNT

The first step to open a stock broker account is to determine that
you desire to invest in stocks as your financial mechanism to
make money, increase your wealth or live comfortable.

Your second step is you determine the money amount that you are able to invest in the stock market. This money sum should be separate from your money that is required to live on. You must realize there is an opportunity to make money, but you have potential to lose part or all your money.

Third step is to assure you have the sufficient free time to complete stock research and to complete stock market purchase and sell trade transactions through your broker.

Fourth you determine your stock market investment strategy goals. These are (1) net flat dollar $ profit, (2) % percent return on your investment, (3) when to sell a stock at a loss and (4) when do you want to withdraw money.

Fifth step is you decide to complete all of your (investor) stock purchase and sell trade transactions as on-line (computer or cell phone) broker transactions which has a lower stock broker commission cost or a stock broker assisted transaction that has a higher commission cost.

Sixth step is you have a computer, lap top or cell phone with a stock broker program for access to complete your on-line trades, stock research and stock market prices. A computer is preferred to use with a Stock Investing Game Plan Sell After Earnings Report trading method due to you have your stock Work Sheet and Computer Spread Sheet sheets that are best completed on a computer. It is important to have access to TV business stations that issue stock alert up-dates and have on-time stock symbol ticker tape.

Seventh step is you develop a stock broker list that you would consider as stock broker candidates to become your stock broker. A list of potential stock broker individuals or firms can be obtained from the internet, telephone directory, newspaper or friend's broker. (See Exhibit 2 – 2)

Eighth step is from computer internet research, friends or stock broker meetings to determine what type of stock investment strategy that matches your life style, best fits your investment money sum, matches your stock market investment goals, matches your time to allocate to financial and stock research and have available computer equipment and cell phone. Also, how do you handle dividends from stocks such as to your broker account, reinvest in the company stock or sent to your residence.

EXHIBIT 2 – 2

STOCK BROKER FIRMS
ALLY INVESTMENT
CHARLES SCHWAB
E TRADE
FIDILITY
INTERACTIVE BROKERW
MERRILL EDGE
ROBIN HOOD
T D AMERITRADE
TRADE STATION

Ninth step is to finalize your selected stock investment strategy. Tenth is with all the above information to set-up a visit with your selected potential stock brokers. During each stock broker visit you obtain answers to your key questions. These questions are (a) stock purchase and sell transaction fee cost includes your on-line fee as base and per contract and sell exchange fees, (b) required stock broker account money to maintain as a minimum, (c) available stock research and computer screens, (d) available free stock market stock training for on-line trading and stock broker program, (e) number of years in business, (f) buy and hold cost for you (an individual) to control the account purchases and sales or stock broker controlled account with its required annual fee calculation such as account end of year money value (g) broker stock account type such as cash or margin, day stock trading or pattern day stock trading account restrictions and requirements, (h) ability to trade stock with extend hours before stock market open, during regular stock trading hours and after stock market closes hours, (i) free stock broker cell phone app to complete stock purchase and sell transactions, (j) stock broker help telephone numbers, (k) stock broker stock trading program training and seminars, (l) after a stock sell transaction when is the money available to you and (m) how to handle dividends such as reinvest in the corporate stock or receive cash in your account or direct to your resident address.   Other considerations are checking account, loan account and local offices in your vacation area or family member residence area.

Open Your Stock Broker Account

After you have finalized your stock broker firm selection, then you are ready for your money transfer to your stock account in your selected stock broker firm, complete the necessary paper documentation, stock broker computer program transferred to your compute/lap top and cell phone along with passwords and identification. It is very important to complete your stock broker program training, paper purchase and sell trade transactions through your broker account. After you feel comfortable with the stock trading activities, then you are ready to start actual stock trading.

Basic On-Line Stock Broker Account Types
A stock trading account options are (1) you complete (an individual investor) on-line computer or cell phone trading account purchase and sell transactions with a stock broker or broker firm. An on-line broker trade commission cost is an estimated $5.00 per purchase transaction that is completed to your cash or margin stock broker account or (2) stock broker completed (assisted) stock trading account that has a stock broker complete your stock purchase and sell trade transactions at a commission cost of estimated $20.00 per transaction. When on-line stock trading account fee is compared to a broker completed trading fee, an on line stock trading account has the lowest broker trading commission by $10.00 (See Exhibit 2 - 3).

Cash Stock Broker Account
A cash stock trading broker account has you (investor) to complete all stock purchase trading transactions (including broker purchase commissions and exchange sell fees) for cash value that is available in your stock broker account. When you complete a cash stock purchase transaction, your stock purchase market value is added to your stock market portfolio market value and minus your stock purchase price and broker commission. After a cash stock sell transaction the sell cash value is added to your broker account less exchange fees that increases your portfolio cash balance.

Margin Stock Broker Account
A margin stock trading broker account has you (investor) complete all stock trading transactions (including commissions and

exchange fees) for your broker account cash value plus margin stock borrowing amount from a stock broker that is available in your stock broker account. When you complete a margin stock purchase transaction, your stock purchase market value is added to your stock market portfolio market value and minus your stock purchase price and stock broker commissions. After a margin stock sell transaction the sell cash value is added to your broker account (cash value plus margin borrowing amount) less exchange fees that increases your portfolio account cash balance. (See Exhibit 2 – 4)

EXHIBIT 2 – 3

STOCK BROKER COMMISSION & EXCHANGE FEES

STOCK TRADE COMPLETED BY BROKER

SHARE INVEST	$ SHARE	TOTAL COST	LESS COMMISSION	LESS EXCHANGE FEES	NET PORTFOLIO INCREASE
500	$50	$25,000	$20	$1.00	$24,979

STOCK TRADE COMPLETED BY YOU ON-LINE

SHARE INVEST	$ SHARE	TOTAL COST	LESS COMMISSION	LESS EXCHANGE FEES	NET PORTFOLIO INCREASE
500	$50	$25,000	$10.00	$ 1.00	$24,989.

STOCK TRADE COMPLETED BY YOU ON-LINE OR CELL PHONE ADVANTAGE $10.00

Stock Trading Extended Hours
When extended hour trading stock broker account is compared to a regular hour stock trading account, an extended stock trading account feature extends your ability to complete stock purchase and sell trade transactions during a trade day. A stock broker extended stock trading hours options are During the Regular Trading Day Hours, Before Market Opens Hours and After Market Closes Hours.

A Stock Broker Regular Hours stock trading account is a stock broker account that allows you (investor) during a market trading day to complete purchase and sell trade transactions between 900 to 400. Stock Broker Extended Hours stock trading account is a stock broker account that allows you (investor) to complete stock purchase and sell trade transactions before the market opens at 930 AM ET.

The Before Market Opens hours feature allows you to complete stock trade transactions from 705 to 925 AM ET. The After Market closes at 400, After Market Closes hours feature allows you (investor) to complete stock purchase and sell trade transactions from 405 to 800 PM ET.

Cell Phone Stock Trading
Your having an on-line computer/lap top or cell phone app stock trading program allows you to complete stock purchase and sell trade transactions over the internet (from any location) to your stock broker account. All stock purchase and sell trade transactions values are updated onto your (investor) portfolio on cell phone, computer and broker program. When compared to a stock broker assisted stock transaction, on-line computer or cell phone app has a lower stock broker commission to complete a stock purchase and sell trade transactions.

EXHIBIT 2 – 4

BROKER ACCOUNT TYPES

CASH ACCOUNT NO MINIMUM CASH BALANCE

DAY 1	DAY 10
$50,000 CASH AVAILABLE TO TRADE	PORTFOLIO ABC STOCK = $20,000 XYS STOCK = $10,000 DEF STOCK = $10,000 AVAILABLE TO TRADE = $10,000

MARGIN ACCOUNT WITH $5,000 MINIMUM CASH BALANCE

DAY 1		DAY 10
$50,000 CASH AVAILABLE TO TRADE & MAINTAIN $5,000 MARGIN BALANCE	PORTFOLIO ABC STOCK = $20,000 XYS STOCK = $10,000 DEF STOCK = $10,000 GHI STOCK = $15,000 MARGIN BALANCE = - $5,000 $5,000 MARGIN REQUIRED BALANCE NEED $5,000 NEW MONEY OR SELL STOCK	PORTFOLIO SETTLED MARGIN CALL SOLD $10,000 ABC STOCK FROM PORTFOLIO ABC STOCK = $10,000 XYS STOCK = $10,000 DEF STOCK = $10,000 GHI STOCK = $15.000 MARGIN BALANCE = $5,000

Stock Investing Game Plan Sell After Earnings Report A Stock Trading Method Cell Phone Trading In Extended Hours
If your cell phone has your broker extended hours trading app (trade stocks in the morning between 705 to 925 or trade stocks in the afternoon between 405 to 800), then with extended hours trading app you can trade a stock (s) to take advantage of a preferred stock market stock price. This means your stock trading opportunities with extended hours trading are if a market stock price is at your preferred or profitable stock price, (1) then you purchase a stock through your broker or (2) then you sell a stock through your broker.

With Stock Investing Game Plan Sell After Earnings Report A Stock Trading Method and extended hours trading app you are watching CNBC TV or access a friends computer to view on Yahoo and you realize that a stock price has a stock market preferred or profitable stock price, then on your cell phone app you can have a stock broker complete a stock trade transaction and secure the profit.

It has occurred on several occasions to the author that a stock market price reaches a preferred or profitable stock price and during the next day regular hour stock trading session the stock market price has a non- preferred or profitable stock price. (See Exhibit 2 – 5)

Exhibit 2 – 5 Cell Phone Broker Trading

From Charles Schwab

CHAPTER 3

VARIOUS STOCK INVESTMENT STRATEGIES

Stock Market Investment Strategies
A stock market investment strategy through a stock broker firm with on-line computer stock trading is your methodology to complete your stock purchase or sell transactions that meet your investment profit goals or objectives.

The various stock review, stock selection and purchase/sell transactions or investment strategies are
(1) Seat Of Pants, Throwing Darts Or Random Stock Selection
Seat of your pants, throwing darts at a dart board and random selection is a stock investment strategy is not considered for you or a modern stock investor. You select a stock with little or no research and complete through your broker stock purchase transaction and sell transactions with little or thought/research process. With this investment strategy, you complete your stock purchase and sell transactions through your broker.   Examples: are a person likes a stock name or a friend gave a stock name, (2) Day Trading Day Trading is stock investing method that has you complete stock and stock market research to determine stocks to purchase and sell through a broker within a trading day regular trade hours. A day trader completes one, several or multiple stock purchase and sell transactions through a broker within one trade day.   With this strategy, a day trader from these sell trade transactions has available money to complete the next day stock purchase trades through a broker. It is noted with a day trading strategy that most broker firms have certain restrictions and broker account maintenance requirements. Example is an investor purchases ABC stock in the morning and later in the afternoon sells ABC stock,
(3) Buy & Hold
Buy & Hold is a stock market investing method that has you purchase and hold stocks or your appointed stock broker purchase and hold stocks. Usually you hold your stocks for a long time period (usually more than one year) and you do not sell stock shares as a stock market price fluctuates.   Buy and hold stock investment options are

(a) stock broker controlled (appointed broker) stock purchase and sell transactions. With a stock broker buy and hold option an investor grants a broker the authority (not to consult with you an investor) to complete stock buy and sell transactions. All stock broker commission and exchange fees are deducted from your portfolio (See Exhibit 3 - 1). You are responsible stock trading profits/losses, trading income tax and you receive all dividends to your portfolio. Per your stock broker contract you are charge a compensation fee for a stock broker control option which is usually 1.5% of your end of year portfolio value or
(b) individual investor, you control buy and hold option you complete all stock purchase and sell transactions through your broker (See Exhibit 3 - 2). Also, you are responsible stock trading profits or losses, trading income tax and you receive all dividends to your portfolio.

With both buy and hold investment options, you pay a stock brokerage purchase commission and exchange fee for each stock round trip (purchase and sell) transaction,
(3) Pattern Day Trading Pattern Trading is stock investing method that has you complete one or several stock purchase and sell transactions through your broker over a short time period of several stock trading days. Some broker firms have account restrictions and maintenance requirements. Example is an investor purchases ABC stock on Monday and later in the same week on Thursday sells ABC stock,
(4) Momentum Trading Another similar stock investing approach to stock day trading is momentum trading. With the momentum investing approach, you (an investor) through your purchase a stock at a high market price and through your broker sell the same stock at a higher market price.
(5) Stock Investing Game Plan Sell After Earnings Report a stock trading method
Stock Investing Game Plan Sell After Earnings Report a stock trading method is similar to momentum investing but there are differences. The differences are (a) that you do not have to develop stock price movement trends to identify qualified stocks and (b) your Stock Investing Game Plan Sell After Earnings Report a stock trading method stocks that have been researched and determined as qualified stocks and (5) Stock Investing Game Plan Sell After Earnings Report A Stock Trading Method Stock

Investing Game Plan Sell After Earnings Report a stock trading method is a stock investing strategy that has you create a qualified stock investment list. This list is based on your stock research (free on the internet) that includes each stock estimated digital earnings release month, digital earnings release day of month, alpha character trading day earnings release time, from a calendar earnings release alpha character day of the week, financial analyst stock ranking and if available from your Stock Investing Game Plan Sell After Earnings Report a stock trading method past history (completed stock Work Sheets). You complete stock research on a stock Initial and Final Note Pad to determine the best qualified stocks with earnings releases for a specific stock trading day. From your stock Final Note Pad, you transfer all the stock information onto an earnings release day stock Work Sheet. With this qualified stock list, 3 to 4 trading or additional days prior to a stock earnings release date, you complete your stock purchase transaction through your broker. On your stock Work Sheet and Computer Spread Sheet from your broker your enter a break-even stock purchase market price that has you add a broker flat commission fee and exchange fee to the broker stock purchase price. A stock reports its quarterly corporate earnings on the earnings release day with a positive earnings report, positive earnings per share and strong management corporation guidance. This feature has a stock market price increase above your break-even purchase price to match your investment goals and you sell the stock through your stock broker at a profit. If a corporation miss earnings, earning per share and give poor management future guidance, this usually a stock market price decrease below your break-even purchase price, then you sell your stock through your stock broker at a loss or hold the stock for the next trading session.

Stock Investment Strategy Comparison
A stock investment plan with a broker completing all stock purchase transactions and sell transactions profits are very simple for you (an investor). From selling stocks, the profits are used to purchase next day earnings release stock or new additional stocks. Our example has three different investment money sums and the results are shown in (See Exhibit 3 - 2). Broker controlled plan with $25,000 invested money plan provided end of year

$1,233 flat dollar profit or 5% return on invested money. The $50,000 invested money plan provided end of year $2,496 flat dollar profit or 5% return on invested money.   The $100,000 invested money plan provided end of year $5,023 flat dollar profit or 5% return on invested money.

A stock investment plan with you (an individual investor) to all complete on-line all stock purchase transactions and sell transactions through a broker. The profit is used to purchase new earnings release or additional stocks. Our example has three different investment money sums and results are shown (See Exhibit 3 - 1).

You complete all trades on-line through a broker plan. The $25,000 invested money plan provided end of year $1,632 flat dollar end or 5% return on invested money. The $100,000 invested money plan provided end of year $3,296 flat dollar profit or 5% return on invested money.   The $50,000 invested money plan provided end of year
$6,622 flat dollar or 5% return on invested money.

 When we compare the two stock investment strategies with three investment money amounts, the conclusions are end of year flat dollar return and % percent return on invested money that has the individual investor plan with end of year flat $ dollar profit and a higher % percent return on invested money higher than a broker controlled investment plan.

EXHIBIT 3 – 1

STOCK TRADING METHOD BROKER TRADE RESULTS

WITH $25,000 INVESTMENT MONEY

QTER INVEST $	PER SHR $	SHRE PURC #	EARN SHR $	TO PTFLIO $	TRADE COST $	NET PROFIT $	PTFLIO VLE $	RETURN VLE %
$25,000	343.22	73	5.49	400	10	390		
$25,390	338.84	75	4.62	346	10	336		
$25,726	341.12	75	12.65	916	10	906		
$26,632	354.61	75	5.59	420	10	410	$26,632 (*)	$1,233 .05

(*) $399   LESS 1.5% BROKER FEE ON PORTOLIO END OF YEAR BALANCE

WITH $50,000 INVESTMENT MONEY END

QTER INVEST $	PER SHR $	SHRE PURC #	EARN SHR $	TO PTFLIO $	TRADE COST $	NET PROFIT $	PTFLIO VLE $	RETURN VLU %
$50,000	343.22	146	5.49	800	10	790		
$50,790	338.84	150	4.62	693	10	683		
$51,472	341.12	151	12.65	916	10	1,823		
$53,296	354.61	150	5.59	840	10	830	$52,496 (*)	$2,496 .05

(*) $799   LESS 1.5% BROKER FEE ON PORTOLIO END OF YEAR BALANCE

WITH $100,000 INVESTMENT MONEY

QTER INVEST $	PER SHR $	SHRE PURC #	EARN SHR $	TO PTFLIO $	TRADE COST $	NET PROFIT $	PTFLIO VLE $	RETURN VLE %
$50,000	343.22	146	5.49	800	10	1,590		
$50,790	338.84	150	4.62	693	10	1,375		
$51,472	341.12	151	12.65	916	10	3,657		
$53,296	354.61	150	5.59	840	10	1,671	$105,023(*)	$5,023 .05

(*) $1,599   LESS 1.5% BROKER FEE ON PORTOLIO END OF YEAR BALANCE

EXHIBIT 3 – 2

STOCK TRADING METHOD INVESTOR TRADE RESULTS

WITH $25,000 INVESTMENT MONEY

QTER INVEST $	PER SHR $	SHRE PURC #	EARN SHR $	TO PTFLIO $	TRADE COST $	NET PROFIT $	PTFLIO VALUE $	RETURN VALUE %
$25,000	343.22	73	5.49	400	10	390		
$25,390	338.84	75	4.62	346	10	336		
$25,726	341.12	75	12.65	916	10	906		
$26,632	354.61	75	5.59	420	10	410	$26,632	$1,632 .07

WITH $50,000 INVESTMENT MONEY

QTER INVEST $	PER SHR $	SHRE PURC #	EARN SHR $	TO PTFLIO $	TRADE COST $	NET PROFIT $	PTFLIO VALUE $	RETURN VALUE %
$50,000	343.22	146	5.49	800	10	790		
$50,790	338.84	150	4.62	693	10	1,375		
$51,472	341.12	151	12.65	916	10	3,657		
$53,296	354.61	150	5.59	840	10	1,671	$53,296	$3,296 .07

WITH $100,000 INVESTMENT MONEY

QTER INVEST $	PER SHR $	SHRE PURC #	EARN SHR $	TO PTFLIO $	TRADE COST $	NET PROFIT $	PTFLIO VALUE $	RETURN VALUE %
$50,000	343.22	146	5.49	800	10	790		
$50,790	338.84	150	4.62	693	10	1,375		
$51,472	341.12	151	12.65	916	10	3,657		
$53,296	354.61	150	5.59	840	10	1,671	$53,296	$3,296 .07

CHAPTER 4

STOCK MARKET RISK FACTORS

Stock Market Price General Marco & Micro Risk Factors
There are numerous micro and macro domestic and international business (Cycles and GNP Statements), economic (Federal Reserve Interest Rates, Inflation or Recession), social and political (Budget or Grid Lock) risk factors that affect a stock earnings per share and stock market price. Most of these risk factors are beyond your (an individual investor) control and have an impact on all stock market prices.

   If there is a bull stock market, then there are usually stock price increases. If there is a bear stock market, then there are usually stock price decreases. All these stock market risk factors create a possible stock market price impact that could cause you to lose part or all of your invested money.

Individual Stock Investing Game Plan Sell After Earnings Report A Stock Trading Method Factors
A corporation individual stock price risk factors have a direct impact on a stock market and individual stock price. A Stock Investing Game Plan Sell After Earnings Report a stock trading method risk factors are
1. Corporation Total Earnings or Sales
 If corporation reported total earnings/sales that were weak or missed analyst estimates, a stock market price declines and creates a potential for you to sell your stock to lose part or all of your stock investment. If corporate reported earnings beat analyst estimates, then a stock market price increases and you have potential to sell your stock at a profit and increase your money,
2. Reported Earnings Per Share
If corporate reported earnings per share were weak or below analyst estimates, a stock market price declines and you have a potential sell your n stock at a lose part or all of your stock investment. If corporate reported earnings release beat analyst estimates, then a stock market price increases and you have potential to sell your stock and increase your money,

3. Corporate Management Guidance Or Future Sales Projection If a corporate management forecasts slow sales/earnings due to inflation, rising interest rates, domestic and international economic, social and political conditions and product competitive industry market, then a stock market price declines and you have a potential sell your stock to lose a part or all of your stock investment.   If a corporation management forecasts strong earnings/growth due to controlled inflation, low interest rates, domestic and international economic, social and political conditions and product dominance in the industry/ market, then a stock market price increase and you have potential to sell at a profit stock at a profit and increase your money.

4. Bull or Bear Market Sentiment.

If a corporation reports earnings in a bull market, then usually a stock market price increases and you have potential to sell your stock at a profit and increase your money.   If a corporation reports earnings in a bear market, then usually a stock market price decreases and you have

a potential sell your stock to lose a part or all of your stock investment.

CHAPTER 5

STOCK INVESTING GAME PLAN SELL AFTER EARNINGS A STOCK TRADING METHOD REPORT STEPS

Stock Investing Game Plan Sell After Earnings Report A Stock Trading Method Defined

Stock Investing Game Plan Sell After Earnings Report a stock trading method is a stock investing strategy that is simple and does not require charting or additional computer investments. It has you (an investor) develop a qualified stock list that is based on your stock research. Your stock research includes financial company's estimated stock earnings release trading month, earnings release day of week, earnings release trading day of the month and earnings release time of trading day and analyst earnings forecast. After completing your stock research you determine the best qualified stocks for a specific earnings release trading month and earnings release trading day of the month with its earnings release trading day report time. From your stock Note Pad list, these qualified stocks and each anticipated purchase quantity are listed on stock Work Sheet.

With your qualified earnings release day of a month on a stock Work Sheet, 3 to 4 or additional trading days prior to a stock earnings release date you complete through a broker your stock purchase transaction. On earnings release day of a month Work Sheet and Computer Spread Sheet enter into your computer the stock list and each stock break-even share purchase (break-even) price.   A stock purchase (break-even) transaction price is your combined broker stock purchase price, stock broker commission and exchange fees.

After a stock releases its earnings with a positive (beat) earnings release, positive earnings per share figure and strong corporate guidance, a stock market price increases above your purchase price to match your investment goals and you sell your stock through a stock broker to make a profit. If a stock earnings release has a miss, negative earnings per share and poor corporate management guidance, your stock market price decreases below your purchase price that does not match your investment goals. To minimize your loss you sell your stock through a stock broker at a market price for a loss or wait for the next stock trading session that could have a slight stock market price increase and you sell your stock through a stock broker.

What To Do Before Trading Stocks With Stock Investing Game Plan Sell After Earnings Report A Stock Trading Method

There are numerous steps you complete before you start trading stocks with the Stock Investing Game Plan Sell After Earnings Report a stock trading method.   These steps (See Exhibit 5 - 1) are to

(1) first step is to establish a stock broker account and transfer your money into the account. To assure you are familiar with your stock broker stock trading program you complete paper trading purchase and sell transactions. Also, you set your investment goals. After you have mastered your broker trading program, you are ready to purchase and sell stocks for money,

(2) second step, to complete stock research to obtain corporate stock list of symbols that you write onto a stock Initial Note Pad. These symbols are obtained from reading articles, news clips, TV programs, cell phone, friends or other reports and your past month completed stock Work Sheets,

(3) next step, you use from one or several financial company stock market reports (earnings and calendar of earnings reports). From these reports on your stock Initial Note Pad you write next to the stock symbols (a) stock earnings release month, earnings release trading day of month and earnings release trading day time, (b) analyst estimated earnings ranking and other important information.   With this stock information you review your stock list and refine your list to your qualified stock candidates by the analyst ranking that you consider qualified stocks. The stocks with their information are easily transferred from a stock Initial Note Pad onto your stock Final Note Pad, (4) for each earnings release day of month you create a stock Final Note Pad for your qualified stock candidates. A company (symbol) earnings date information is obtain from one of the following financial company reports. These are (a) Zacks Earnings Calendar, Earnings Report or Stock Overview & Earnings page, (b) Yahoo Earnings Calendar, Company Quote Page, (c) broker such as Schwab Company Research Page, (d) GOOGL/NASDAQ/ZACKs earnings page, (e) Bloomberg Calendar of Earnings or your past Work Sheets.

A stock Final Note Pad for each earnings release day of a month has you automatically arrange stocks in a sequential order that has a stock with the earnings release lowest digital month as first month and a last stock with the earnings release highest digital month. As you write stocks onto a stock Final Note Pad you have stocks grouped by a trading day earnings release time of day notation such as the BM group first, DH group second and AF group as last, (5) next step you transfer one trading day earnings release stocks from your Final Note Pad onto your stock Work Sheet with the same earnings release day of a month. This means each earnings release day of a month has one stock Work Sheet page. Your stock transfer is from your stock Final Note Pad to your stock Work Sheet. In this transfer you automatically list stocks with BM first, then stocks with DH second and last stocks with AF. This Work Sheet stock arrangement has an earnings release day of a month stocks arranged to match a stock market earnings release time in a trading day. From a calendar you enter into your computer each stocks alpha character work day notation, (6) next refresh yourself with your stock trading goals or profit standards, (7) to learn Stock Investing Game Plan Sell After Earnings Report trading method, you transfer qualified stocks from your computer stock Work Sheet to your computer stock Computer Spread Sheet, (8) on your computer you complete your paper stock purchase and sell trade transactions. You complete several stock market prices to assure your familiar with the stock final sell price.   When you feel comfortable with the Stock Investing Game Plan Sell After Earnings Report a stock trading method, you are ready to complete money stock trade transactions. Since these paper trades are for qualified Stock Investing Game Plan Sell After Earnings Report a stock trading method stocks with an earnings release dated stock Work Sheet and save the stock purchase and sell transactions prices and your trading performance. This saved stock Work Sheet feature becomes a stock research source, transfer a month earnings release day stocks and information from your stock Spread Sheet to your stock Work Spread Sheet.

You are ready to start Stock Investing Game Plan Sell After Earnings Report trading method stock trading for money starts in your computer as you enter a broker stock purchase price and you enter a sell stock recent market price. With a sell price your computer calculates your potential profit or loses above your broker break-even purchase price that you match to your investment goal. If you have a potential profit, then you complete a stock sell transaction through your broker. After your broker notifies you of your stock sell transaction price, you enter a stock net cash amount into your stock Computer Spread Sheet. Your computer calculates your actual stock trading performance. After you enter your broker stock purchase and sell transactions prices into your Work Sheet, you remove all completed stock transactions from your Computer Spread Sheet, (10) on your stock Work Sheet your computer shows your stock broker purchase and sell transactions and calculates your stock trading performance and (11) your completed stock Work Sheet that is identified with an earnings release trading day of a month becomes your future stock research source.

Your Stock Broker Account & Account Features
Your first step to trade stocks with a Stock Investing Game Plan Sell After Earnings Report a stock trading method is to establish a cash or margin stock broker account.

     To complete timely stock trades and maximize your profits you trade on-line to your stock broker account program, you require several features. The first feature is to have an on-line computer and cell phone app that allows you to complete from your home computer or anywhere with your cell phone a stock trading transaction over the internet to your broker stock account. All completed stock transactions are updated onto your stock broker account, your computer program and cell phone. When compared to a broker assisted stock transaction, on-line computer or cell phone app has a lower stock broker commission to complete a stock trade transaction.

     The second feature is your stock broker account should have extended hours stock trading features. This feature allows you with the opportunity to complete stock trade transactions before the market opens at 930 AM ET or from 705 AM ET to trade to 905 AM ET, during regular trading hours between 930 AM ET to 400 PM ET and after the stock market closes at 400 PM ET for you to complete stock trades from 405 PM ET to 800 PM ET. Extended hours feature allows you to take advantage of a stock price market increase before or after regular trading hours and you do not wait for regular hours trading time. If have stock reports BEFORE OR AFTER regular trading hours and has a price increase, then this means you have potential to complete a stock sell transaction to obtain your desired stock trade price at a market price that enhances your profits.

The third feature is to set your stock investment goals that are based stock price increase or profit as a (1) net flat dollar profit per stock, (2) percentage increase as a return on your stock investment and (3) with a loss to cut your portfolio loses.

Stock Investing Game Plan Sell After Earnings Report A Stock Trading Method Investing Components

Your Stock Investing Game Plan Sell After Earnings Report a stock trading method investment strategy has many components. Your first two components are main factors in your Stock Investing Game Plan Sell After Earnings Report a stock trading method. These components have an impact on your stock trading results and are your (1) broker completed stock purchase price and (2) broker completed stock sell price.

Your stock investing steps are (1) you establish your stock investing goals or objectives. These are (a) net flat dollar $ profit or (b) % return on your investment money, (2) you establish your company stock share quantity to purchase each transaction and (3) you determine your different company stocks to purchase. These options are (a) designed with a standard approach or stock purchase quantity for different company stock shares that do not change per a stock market price or (b) designed with a flexible approach stock purchase quantity change or investor's desire for different company stocks quantity that are determine by a stock market high price or your available investment funds.

Investing Game Plan Sell After Earnings Report A Stock Trading Method How Does Work

Stock Investing Game Plan Sell After Earnings Report a stock trading method is a stock investing strategy that has several steps. These steps are (1) to establish your stock investing goals and objectives, (2) with various tools complete your stock research for a qualified candidate stock investment list, (3) to complete your selected stock purchase and sell trade transactions and (4) to complete your stock investment records.

EXHIBIT 5 – 1

STOCK INVESTING GAME PLAN SELL AFTER EARNINGS REPORT (SIGPSAER) A STOCK TRADING METHOD STOCK TRADING FLOW CHART

REFRESH YOUR STOCK INVESTMENT GOALS

↓

FROM STOCK MARKET RESEARCH SOURCES DEVELOP SIGPSAER DATE TRADING METHOD INITIAL NOTE PAD WITH STOCK SYMBOLS OR CORPORATE NAMES

↓

FOR EACH EARNINGS RELEASE MONTH, DAY OF MONTH, TRADING DAY RELEASE TIME HAS A MONTH STOCK FINAL SIGPSAER NOTE PAD SHEET & PER YOUR ANALYST EARNINGS RANK ADD OR ELIMINATE STOCKS FROM LIST

↓

SIGPSAER FINAL NOTE PAD FROM STOCK RESEARCH SOURCES STOCK EARNINGS RELEASE MONTH, DAY, TRADING DAY RELEASE TIME & ANALYST RANKING. TRANSFER TO FIRST MONTH & NEXT TWO MONTHS TO SIGPSAER TRADING METHOD WORK SHEETS

↓

TITLE YOUR SIGPSAER WORK SHEET WITH STOCK PURCHASE DATE & EARNING RELEASE DATE CLEAR SPACE. VERIFY AND QUALIFY YOU CANDIDATE STOCK LIST. ADD STOCK TO SIGPSAER EARNINGS RELEASE DAY WORK SHEET. EACH STOCK HAS EARNINGS RELEASE DIGITAL MONTH WITH SPACE FOR ALPHA CHARACTER RELEASE TIME IN TRADING DAY AS (BH), (RH) & (AF) & DIGITAL EARNINGS RELEASE DAY OF MONTH & ALPHA CHARACTER DAY OF WEEK. LISTED BY THE LOWEST MONTH FIRST & TRADING DAY TIME TO REPORT WITH FIRST GROUP AS BM, SECOND GROUP AS DH & LAST GROUP AS AF

↓

FROM EACH EARNINGS RELEASE DATE TRADING DAY SIGPSAER WORK SHEET TRANSFER STOCK DATA TO SIGPSAER COMPUTER SPREAD SHEET & HOLD PARITAL COMLETE FILE EARNINGS RELEASE DAY WORK SHEET FOR LATER COMPUTER SPREAD SHEET STOCK PURCHASE & SELL PRICE UPDATE

↓

PURCHASE STOCK ADD SHARE QUANTTY & PER SHARE $ PRICE TO SIGPSAER COMPUTER SPREAD SHEET & SIGPSAER EARNING RELEASE DAY WORK SHEET

↓

ON EARNINGS RELEASE DAY FROM CORPORATE EARNINGS, EPS & MANAGEMENT GUIDANCE IF PRICE INCREASE MATCHES YOUR INVESTMENT GOALS SELL STOCK ADD STOCK PER SHARE $ PRICE TO SIGPSAER COMPUTER SPREAD SHEET, COMPUTER CALCULATES PROFIT OR LOSS & ADD TO COMPUTER SIGPSAER COMPUTER SPREAD SHEET & TO SIGPSAER EARNINGS RELEASE DAY PARTIAL COMPLETE WORK SHEET

↓

FILE EACH EARNING RELEASE DAY OF MONTH COMPLETED SIGPSAER METHOD EARNINGS RELEASE DAY WORK SHEET

Your Stock Investing Game Plan Sell After Earnings Report a stock trading method first step is to assure that you have strong stock investing goals and objectives. These are for each stock purchase price to sell each stock above a stock purchase price at a (1) net flat dollar $ profit and (2) to sell at a percent % return on your invested money.

EXHIBIT 5 – 2

STOCK INVESTING GAME PLAN SELL AFTER EARNINGS REPORT A STOCK TRADING METHOD INVESTMENT GOALS

FLAT DOLLAR $ INVESTMENT PROFIT
FLAT DOLLAR INVESTMENT PROFIT GOAL = $2,000	
STOCK SHARES = 500 AT $10 PER SHARE	$5,000
STOCK MARKET PRICE = $15 PER SHARE	$7,500
FLAT DOLLAR INVESTMENT PROFIT	$2,500
SELL THE SHARES	

PERCENT 5% RETURN ON INVESTED DOLLARS $
FLAT DOLLAR INVESTMENT PROFIT GOAL = %5	
STOCK SHARES = 500 AT $10 PER SHARE	$5,000
STOCK MARKET PRICE = $12 PER SHARE	$6,000
FLAT DOLLAR INVESTMENT PROFIT	$1,000
PERCENTAGE RETURN = $,1000/$5,000	20%
SELL THE SHARES	

The second step is stock research with a stock Initial Note Pad and Final Note Pad. Using a stock Note Pad concept is a two step process. The first step is a basic stock research step from stock market or financial market print, TV, cell phone, internet or friend news that has you list onto each stock symbol or corporate name on your stock Initial Note Pad. A stock Initial Note Pad is a random arranged stock symbol list. From stock broker or financial companies stock
reports to each stock symbol you add its earnings release trading month digits and day of month digits and earnings release trading day time. (See Exhibit 5 – 3)

The next step is from a stock Initial Note Pad list to develop a stock Final Note Pad. (See Exhibit 5 – 4) You have one Final Note Pad for each earnings release day of a month. On a stock Final Note Pad, you arrange stocks from the present (lowest numbered) earnings release trading month and earnings release

EXHIBIT 5 – 3

STOCK INVESTING GAME PLAN SELL AFTER EARNINGS REPORT
A STOCK TRADING METHOD INITIAL NOTE PAD

XYZ
TOL
BA
AMZN
DER
TEAM
SPLUK
XLINX

ALL STOCK SYMBOLS AND INFORMATION RANDOMLY LISTED & HAND
WRITTEN (NO CHRONOLOGICAL ORDER) BY DATE FOR EARNINGS RELEASE

trading day of month sequence, to the highest earnings release trading month and earnings release trading day of month sequence. Also, these stocks are grouped by earnings release trading day time. This arrangement has all stocks with abbreviation (BM) grouped together, (DH) grouped together or (AF) grouped together. You provide from a calendar each stock earnings release day of a week alpha notation. Each stock has two financial analyst stock earnings rankings.

Step three is from your stock Final Note Pad you transfer all of your stock data into your computer all of your stock data to your stock Work Sheet. For each earnings release day of a month there is each Stock Investing Game Plan Sell After Earnings Report a stock trading method Work Sheet that has a unique identification of a stock purchase day of the month and earnings release day of the month. On a stock Work Sheet your stocks have arrangement in three groups by earnings release trading day of month and associated earnings release time of day. On your stock Work Sheet, the first stock group has all Before Market Opens (BM) stocks, your second stock group has all During Regular Hours (DH) stocks and your third stock group has all After Market (AF) stocks.

Step four each stock information from your stock Work Sheet computer you transfer to your stock Computer Spread Sheet (See Exhibit 5 –5) Your stock Spread Sheet is your stock trading road map or trading platform. As a stock earnings release occurs and you listen to CNBC TV, Bloomberg TV, cell phone app or Yahoo finance you sources you become aware of a stock earnings release, earnings per share release and corporate management guidance. From these stock earnings alert obtain the latest stock market price. You enter the stock price under a Computer Spread

EXHIBIT 5 – 4

STOCK INVESTING GAME PLAN SELL AFTER EARNINGS REPORT
A STOCK TRADING METHOD FINAL NOTE PAD

XYZ 1/9BM
TOL1/20DH
BA1/30AF
AMZN2/2DH
XLNX2/6AF
DER3/3BM
TEAM3/6DH

HAND WRITTEN BY CHRONOLOGICAL ORDER BY EARNINGS RELEASE DIGITALMONTH WITH TRADING DAY TIME ALPHA CHARACTER ,DIGITAL DAY OF MONTH, STOCK SYMBOL, ALPHA CHARCTER DAY OF WEEK EARNINGS RELEASE AND ESTIMATED RANKING

Sheet stock market price column. After stock market price entry, your computer calculates your potential stock flat dollar $ increase or % return on invested $ dollars. If your stock market price increase matches your investment goals, then you sell your stock through your broker and pocket the profits. If your stock market price decreases that does not match your investment goals, then you sell your stock through your broker at a loss. After you complete your trade transactions, you enter your broker stock purchase and sell trade transaction prices onto your stock Work Sheet that shows your Stock Investing Game Plan Sell After Earnings Report a stock trading method trading performance. On your Computer Spread Sheet you remove all completed stock trade transactions that make space available for the next earnings release day stocks.

Step five is to track your Stock Investing Game Plan Sell After Earnings Report a stock trading method stock trading performance. To complete a Computer Spread Sheet, each broker stock purchase and sell (market) transaction price is entered onto your Computer Spread Sheet appropriate lines. After your broker stock purchase and sell price entries, your computer calculates and shows your stock profit or loss.

Next you transfer your broker stock purchase and sell and stock trading purchase and sell transaction prices from your stock Computer Spread Sheet to your computer stock Work Sheet.

EXHIBIT 5 - 5

COMPLETE STOCK INVESTING GAME PLAN SELL AFTER EARNINGS REPORT A STOCK TRADING METHOD COMPUTER SPREAD SHEET

SETTLED FUNDS
DAY TRADING BUYING POWER
AVAILABLE TO TRADE
CASH & BORROWING

(1)	(2)	(3)	(4)	(5)	(6)	(7)	(8)	(9)	(10)	(11)	(12)
DIGITAL											PRTFLIO
MONTH	ALPHA		ANALYST								PRTFLIO
& DAY &	MONTH		STK		STK	STK	STK	STK	STK	STK	MARKET
TRADE	DAY	STOCK	RANK		PRCHSE	BRK EN	MARKET	GN / LS	GN / LS	VALUE	VALUE
TIME	DATE	SYMBOL	(1)	(2)	#	$	$	$	%	$	$
1/9BM	MON	XYZ	3	**	300	75	67.1	7.90	.11	2370	22500
1/20DH	TUES	TOL	2	*	300	85	83.1	1.90	.02	570	25500
1/30AF	WEDS	BA	1	**	300	345	310.1	34.90	.10	10470	103500
2/2DH	MON	AMZN	1	**	200	1377	1339.1	37.90	.03	7580	275400
2/2AF	MON	SPLK	1	**	300	133	12.76	120.24	.90	36072	39900
2/6AF	FRI	XLNX	2	**	300	210	175.11	34.89	.17	10467	63000
3/3BM	THUR	DER	3	*	300	35	43.89	- 8.89	-.25	-2667	10500
3/6DH	THUR	TEAM	2	**	300	97	91.43	5.57	.06	167	29100

MONTH TO DATE 66533   GROSS VALUE 66533 569400
MONTH DATE WITH MARGIN   61643   MARGIN   -4890
NET VALUE   564510

	MONTH	WITH	W MARGIN	NO	
	MARGIN	MARGIN	YTD	MARGIN	YTD
MONTH	$	$	$	$	$

This step (1) you update your stock Computer Spread Sheet computer by removing all sold/completed/past earnings release day stock information and (2) allows you to add the next earnings release day stock information from the next earnings release trading day stock Work Sheet line and to your Computer Spread Sheet.

Step six is your stock record keeping step. In this step you assure that your stock Work Sheet is complete. A stock Work Sheet has your records for a Stock Investing Game Plan Sell After Earnings Report a stock trading method earnings release trading day of the month and becomes you're stock research source.

Digital & Alpha Dates In Stock Investing Game Plan Sell After Earnings Report A Stock Trading Method
A stock estimated earnings release date is a very important Stock Investing Game Plan Sell After Earnings Report a stock trading method component. On your stock Work Sheet and stock Computer Spread Sheet computer, you list each stock earnings release digital month, digital earnings release day of a month and earnings release time during a trading day. Each earnings release trading day time has an alpha character notation. From a calendar you add an earnings release day of week alpha character notation. On your stock Computer Spread Sheet, your stocks are listed in calendar chronological order from the first earnings release day of a month (day one of a month with alpha character notation) to the last earnings release day of a month. Each group is grouped by earnings release time in a trading day. On your stock Work Sheet and stock Computer Spread Sheet, one column is for a stock earnings release digital month and day of a month with some additional space (9/21--). The additional space is for a stock earnings release time in a trading day alpha character notation. Another column has a corporate earnings release alpha day of the week notation from a calendar such as (MON, TUES, WEDS, THURS or FRI). (See Exhibit 5 – 8) A stock earnings release day/date is a calendar date that you must own a stock.

Stock Investing Game Plan Sell After Earnings Report A Stock Trading Method Earnings Release Trading Day Time
Stock Investing Game Plan Sell After Earnings Report a stock trading method earnings release trading day time is a corporation projected trading day time for earnings release such Before Market Opens (BM), During Regular Hours (DH) & After Market Closes (AF).
    A corporation stock estimated earnings release trading day time is another very important stock trading component. You obtain earnings release time for trading day information from a financial company's earnings calendar. The earnings release time in a trading day is entered in your stock Work Sheet and enter in your stock Computer Spread Sheet column with sufficient space for earning release trading time digital date. This feature alerts you to a stock earnings trading day for report time, on your stock

Computer Spread Sheet digital date column adjacent sufficient space is allow for you to add BM (Before Market Opens), During Market Regular Hours (DH) and After Market Closes (AF) (See Exhibit 5 – 9).

Before Market Opens means that a you desire to sell through your stock broker and obtain a stock market price increase due to excellent earnings, then to obtain your stock profit you must have a stock broker account with Extended Hours Trading. This feature allows you to complete trade transactions from 705 PM ET to 925 PM ET or before the market opens at 930 PM ET at the before hours market price to obtain your profits.   If you wait for the market to open, then there is a possibility for a stock price to decrease and you do not obtain your profit.

EXHIBIT 5 – 6

DIGITAL EARNINGS RELEASE TRADING DAY NOTATION
TRADING MONTH AND DAY NOTATION
    MONTH HAS 1, 2, 3, 4, 5, 6, 7, 8, 9, 10, 11, 12
    DAY HAS 1 THRU 31
PLUS PER COMMON STOCK TRADING TIME OF DAY ABBREVIATIONS
    (BM) BEFORE MARKET OPENS
    (DH) DURING REGLAR MARKET HOURS
    (AF) AFTER HOURS
EXAMPLE OCTOBER 12 BEFORE MARKET OPENS
    NOTATION = 10/12BM

ALPHA CHARACTER EARNINGS RELEASE TRADING DAY NOTATION
MONDAY =   MON
TUESDAY =   TUES
WEDSADAY = WEDS
THURSDAY = THUS
 FRIDAY =   FRI

After Market Closes means that a corporation reports earnings in after trading day or reported after 400 AM ET (time stock market closes). If a stock has a large market price increase due to excellent earnings, then to obtain your stock profit you must have a stock broker account with Extended Hours

Trading.   This feature allows you to complete stock sell trade transactions through a broker from 405 AM ET to 800 AM ET or after the market closes at 400 AM ET. If you wait for the next day trading market to open, then there is a possibility for a stock price to decrease and you do not obtain your profit.

Stock broker regular hours trading account is a stock broker account that allows you to complete stock purchase or sell transactions through your stock broker between 900 PM ET and 400 AM ET. Stock broker regular hours trading account is a stock broker account that allows you to complete stock transactions through your broker between from 930 PM ET to 400 AM ET.

On your stock Work Sheet and on your common stock Computer Spread Sheet computer, your stocks are listed in calendar chronological order from the first earnings release month, earnings release trading day of a month date group to the last earnings release trading day of a month by BM, DH & AF. On your stock Work Sheet and stock Computer Spread Sheet computer, a column has each stock earnings release trading day of a month digital notation date and sufficient space to add earnings release time of trading day (9/21BM for Before Open, (9/21DH for During Regular Hours) and (9/21AF) for After Hours). From a calendar in a second column you enter a stock alpha character notation for trading day of a week such as (MON), (TUES), (WEDS), (THUR) & (FRI). This feature keeps a stock trader aware of each stock earnings release day of a week.

Financial Company Analyst Stock Earnings Estimate Or Ranking
In many financial company earnings calendars, an analyst presents a stock earnings release estimate or ranking. An analyst is a person or corporation analyst who has an economic, financial, accounting degree or stock market working experience to mathematically and analytically project a stock future price.   An analyst estimate for future corporate earnings quality is another important stock qualifier factor. On your stock Work Sheet and stock Computer Spread Sheet computer, you enter your selected financial analyst earnings estimates. On your Work Sheet and Computer Spread Sheet computer, there is sufficient space under a financial estimate column for two financial analyst estimates. A financial company's estimated stock earnings quality has direct

impact on your separation of good quality stock candidates from poor quality stock candidates.

GOOGL/NASDAQ/ZACKs analyst stock earnings consensus recommendation is a presented as a colored banner that goes from red (sell or do not purchase) to yellow and to green (purchase or hold). Based on one or a group of analyst projection(s) an indicator is

EXHIBIT 5 - 7

STOCK INVESTING GAME PLAN SELL AFTER EARNINGS REPORT
A STOCK TRADING METHOD TRADING

WITH REGULAR HOURS TRADING	WITH EXTEND HOURS TRADING
NO STOCK TRADING ALLOWED YOU HAVE STOCK ABC & HAS $10.50 PROFIT PER SHARE & YOU HOLD 300 SHARES OF REGULAR HOURS	BEFORE MARKET HOURS TRADING (BM), YOU HAVE STOCK ABC & HAS $10.50 PROFIT PER SHARE & YOU TRADE YOUR 300 SHARES. YOU CAN TRADE FROM 700 EA TM TO 925 EA TM TIME
STOCK TRADING FROM 900 EA TM TO 400 EA TM. YOU TRADE YOUR ABC 300 SHARES AT MKT PRICE THAT IS MORE OR LESS THAN	STOCK TRADING FROM 900 EA TM TO 400 EA TM (DH)
NO STOCK TRADING ALLOWED. XYZ HAS A PROFIT OF $9.50 PER SHARE. YOU HOLD 300 SHARES FOR NEXT DAY TRADING SESSION FOR MORE OR LESS THAN $10.50	AFTER MARKET HOURS TRADING (AF), YOU HAVE 300 XYZ SHARES WITH A PROFIT 0F $9.50 PER SHARE. YOU SELL YOU 300 SHARES AT $9.50 PER SHARE. YOU CAN TRADE FROM 405 EA TM TO 800 EA TM

positioned along a colored banner that indicates a stock earnings quality. With quality of earnings approach, very high quality stocks have an indicator in the middle of a green banner section and medium quality stock earnings indicator at a green banner start. On your Work Sheet line and stock Computer Spread Sheet line, a common stock earnings estimate in a green banner middle receives two stars and an indicator on a green banner start receives one star. With Stock Investing Game Plan Sell After Earnings Report trading method trading method we consider only quality stocks. If a stock with an indicator in the red or yellow banner colored areas, a stock would not be considered as a qualified stock for your Stock Investing Game Plan Sell After Earnings Report a stock trading method (See Exhibit 5 – 8).

Zack's stock earnings report has an analyst estimated earnings report as a numerical or digital presentation. Zack's analyst earnings estimate numerical ranking uses 1, 2, 3, 4, 5 as quality of stock earnings indicator.   With 1 receiving the strongest recommend quality for a stock's earnings and 5 receiving the lowest/weakest quality for a stock's earnings. With quality of stock earnings approach, on your stock Work Sheet or stock Computer Spread Sheet quality stocks have an indicator of 1 would be a strong buy or excellent quality, 2 would be a buy of medium quality and 3 would be hold. In the Stock Investing Game Plan Sell After Earnings Report stock earnings with a stock estimate with 4 or 5 rank is not be consider a qualified stock for your Stock Investing Game Plan Sell After Earnings Report a stock trading method. Since we are considering quality stocks, then a stock with a 4 or 5 ranking are not considered for Stock Investing Game Plan Sell After Earnings Report a stock trading method. Your stock Work Sheet line or stock Computer Spread Sheet line, under stock earnings column a stock would receive a Zack's ranking 1, 2 or 3 (See Exhibit 5 – 8).

Charles Schwab (stock broker firm) stock earnings estimate research or announcement expected is more focused on a stock price. The research shows your stock symbol, earnings release day of the week and trading day earnings release time. The analyst earnings estimate is a group projection that states a projected earnings dollar value with the analyst high and low dollar values along with last quarter earnings estimate.
(See Exhibit 5 – 8)

Investor Use Of Financial Analyst Stock Earnings Estimates Or Rankings
You as an investor have the ability to use one or all financial analyst stock earnings estimates or rankings to help qualify stocks for your Stock Investing Game Plan Sell After Earnings Report a

stock trading method. These qualified stocks will provide you with the opportunity to match or exceed your investment goals.

It has been the author's experience to use Zacks numerical stock earnings rankings and Googl/NASDAQ/Zacks colored coded racking to qualify stocks for investment.   The past experience is based on the analyst earnings estimate or ranking explanation not to qualify for Stock Investing Game Plan Sell After Earnings Report a stock trading method stocks with (1) Zacks 4 that means sell or 5 that means strong sell numerical ranking or (2) GOOGL/NASDAQ/ZACKs red that means do not purchase or yellow that means hold colored racking. Use a combination of Zacks financial stock earnings racking of any stock with 1 (strong buy) or 2 (buy) numerical ranking. This option provides a medium qualified stock number but some degree of risk,

(1) Use a single Zacks financial stock earnings racking of any stock with 1 (strong buy) numerical ranking. This option provides a smaller qualified stock number but a low degree of risk with qualified stocks but medium degree of risk, Use a combination of GOOGL/NASDAQ/Zacks financial stock earnings racking of any stock with mid green color or (2 stars author's notation) purchase or start green color or (a) star author's notation) hold colored ranking. This option provides a medium qualified stock number but some degree of risk and

(2) Use a combined Zacks financial stock earnings racking of any stock with 1 (strong buy) or 2 (buy) numerical ranking and GOOGL/NASDAQ/Zacks financial stock earnings racking of any stock with mid green color or (2 stars author's notation) purchase) or start green color or (1 star author's notation) hold colored ranking. This option provides a small to medium qualified stock number but some degree of risk, Use a combed Zacks financial stock earnings racking of any stock with 1 (strong buy) numerical ranking and GOOGL/NASDAQ/ZACKs financial stock earnings racking of any stock with mid green color or (2 stars author's notation) purchase colored ranking. This option provides a small qualified stock number but some degree of risk.

EXHIBIT 5 – 8

STOCK INVESTING GAME PLAN SELL AFTER EARNINGS REPORT
A STOCK TRADING METHOD STOCK EARNINGS RANKING

ZACKS DIGITAL RANKING
    1 STRONG BUY
     2 BUY
     3 HOLD
     4 SELL
     5 STRONG SELL

GOOGL/NASDAQ/ZACKS COLOR BANNER RANKING

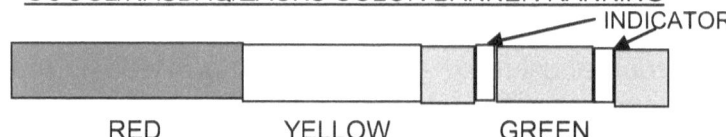

                                                  INDICATOR

    RED   YELLOW   GREEN
    RED = DO NOT PURCHASE
    YELLOW = HOLD
    INDICATOR IN GREEN AT START GETS ONE STAR (*)
    INDICATOR IN GREEN IN MIDDLE GETS TWO STARS (**)

BROKER SCHWAB EPS ESTIMATES
    ESTIMATED NEXT QUARTER EARNINGS $.78
    ESTIMATED NEXT QUARTER EARNINGS RANGE FROM
    SEVERAL ANALYSTS   ESTIMATE = $1.23   HIGH = $1.55
    LOW = $1.03
    LAST YEAR FOR SAME QUARTER $.48 1st.

Past Stock Investing Game Plan Sell After Earnings Report A
Stock Trading Method Work Sheets
Each stock Work Sheet that is identified with (purchase day of a
month and earnings release day of a month) is another stock
qualifying factor. On earnings release day of a month Work Sheet
you enter your stock broker stock share purchase price and sell
(market price). With these stock prices your computer calculates
and states your $ profit or $ loss and % percent return on
investment or stock trading performance. You print paper copy
that becomes a stock research document for future stock
research.

Corporate Earnings Reported Quarterly
Since all corporations are required to issue a corporate earnings
release every 3 months, your stock Work Sheets are records that
show how well each past candidate stock performed in earnings

release month and has potential to repeat in the next month group. With some slight variances due to month calendar days and corporation selected earnings release date, every 3 month stock earnings release schedule has the following month grouping. These 3 groups of 4 months feature has Group 1 months are January, April, July & October, Group 2 months are February, May, August & November and Group 3 months March, June, September & December (See Exhibit 5 – 9).

EXHIBIT 5 – 9

STOCK INVESTING GAME PLAN SELL AFTER EARNINGS A
STOCK TRADING METHOD RELEASE ANTICIPATING STOCK TO
REPEAT EARNINGS BY MONTH GROUPING

GROUP 1	GROUP 2	GROUP 3
JANUARY (1)	FEBRUARY (2)	MARCH (3)
APRIL (4)	MAY (5)	JUNE (6)
JULY (7)	AUGUST (8)	SEPTEMBER (9)
OCTOBER (10)	NOVEMBER (11)	DECEMER (12)

CHAPTER 6

STOCK INVESTING GAME PLAN SELL AFTER EARNINGS REPORT A STOCK TRADING METHOD INITIAL NOTE PAD

Stock Investing Game Plan Sell After Earnings Report A Stock Trading Method Note Pad
The first Stock Investing Game Plan Sell After Earnings Report a stock trading method tool is a stock Initial Note Pad. It is a tool that is a paper sheet and pen and used for your basic stock research (free on the internet). From stock market or financial market printed news, TV, internet or friend news you write (list) each mentioned stock symbol or corporate name onto a stock Initial Note Pad. On a stock Initial Note Pad, your stock symbols have a random arrangement and if available it includes earnings release month and earnings release day of a month. After your first stock Initial Note Pad becomes full, you use a second paper sheet for another stock Initial Note Pad. To best understand an Initial Note Pad, the book has a completed Initial Note Pad. (See Exhibit 6 – 1)

How To Complete A Stock Investing Game Plan Sell After Earnings Report A Stock Trading Method Note Pad
You start your stock Initial Note Pad with a blank paper sheet and pen. As you read or listen to stock news and you become aware of a corporate name or symbol, you add each stock symbol or name is written onto your sock Initial Note Pad.

   Through-out the chapter as we review the various Stock Investing Game Plan Sell After Earnings Report a stock trading method tools, we will use the below stock symbols and corporate names. These are XYZ, TOL, BA, AMZN, DER & TEAM, corporate names Spluk & Xilinx Example: 1/9BH MON XYZ

   Our example has symbols XYZ, TOL, BA, AMZN, DER & TEAM and corporate names Spluk & Xilinx. After you add more stock symbols to your first sheet and it becomes full, then you start a second sheet.

EXHIBIT 6 – 1

STOCK INVESTING GAME PLAN SELL AFTER EARNINGS
RELEASE DATE A STOCK TRADING METHOD INITIAL NOTE
PAD

XYZ
TOL
BA
AMZN
DER
TEAM
SPLUK
XLINX

ALL STOCK SYMBOLS AND INFORMATION RANDOMLY LISTED &
HAND WRITTEN (NO CHRONOLOGICAL ORDER) BY DATE FOR
EARNINGS RELEASE

CHAPTER 7

STOCK INVESTING GAME PLAN SELL AFTER EARNINGS REPORT
A STOCK TRADING METHOD FINAL NOTE PAD

Stock Investing Game Plan Sell After Earnings Report A Stock Trading Method Final Note Pad

The second Stock Investing Game Plan Sell After Earnings Report Method trading method tool is a stock Final Note Pad. A simple and quick technique to complete a Final Note Pad is to have one sheet of paper for each earnings release day of a month. This feature has one page for each earning release day of a month that allows as you transfer stocks from your stock Initial Note to your Final Note Pad for you to quickly locate the appropriate page and write on a stock symbol and other information. A company (symbol) earnings date information is obtain from one of the following (free on the internet) financial company reports. These are (1) Zacks Earnings Calendar, Earnings Report or Stock, (2) Yahoo Calendar of Earnings and Finance Report, (3) Overview & GOOGL/NASDAQ/ZACKs Earnings report, (4) Schwab Company Research Page, (5) Bloomberg Calendar of Earnings or your past Work Sheets.

When you are ready to transfer an earnings release day of a month stocks from a stock Final Note Pad to an earnings release day of a month stock Work Sheet, the stocks transfer is easily and quickly completed.

Part of your stock Final Note Pad activity is to complete some stock research. Your stock research obtains each stock symbol earnings release digital notation for a month, earnings release digital notation day of a month and earnings release during a trading day. On a stock Final Note Pad, you arrange stocks from the present (lowest numbered) earnings release trading month and earnings release trading day of a month sequence to the highest earnings release trading month and earnings release trading day of a month sequence. Such as stock XYZ 9/12 and next is stock ABC 9/13 (See Exhibit 7 – 1).

During your stock research if you become aware of a stock earnings release trading day time, then you indicate an earnings release trading day time. You use an alpha character notation abbreviation (BM), (DH) or (AF) that is placed next to a stock digital earnings release day of a month. Such as stock XYZ 9/12BM, TOL 9/12DH and BA 9/12AF.

How To Complete A Stock Investing Game Plan Sell After Earnings Report A Stock Trading Method Final Note Pad
From your stock Initial Note Pad you transfer all stock information onto your stock Final Note Pad, you list each stock symbol in sequential order with the lowest digital earnings release month first and to the last earnings release trading day of the month. The stock arrangement order is repeated for each earnings release day of a month. Transfer from a stock Initial Note Pad includes all stock symbol information such as earnings release digital month notation
(1 thur 12), earnings release digital day of month (1 thru 31), earnings release day of week alpha character notation and alpha character abbreviation trading day time abbreviations (BM), (DH) or (AF). Example: Final Note Pad all stock information will be hand written and look like 1/9BM MON XYZ.
    If you feel comfortable and leave sufficient space on a stock Initial Note Pad, then you can combine the writing to one page from your stock Final Note Pad you transfer stock digital earnings release month, digital day of a month and earnings release time of trading day alpha character notation to your stock Work Sheet lines.

EXHIBIT 7 – 1

STOCK SELLING GAME PLAN AFTER EARNINGS REPORT
A STOCK TRADING METHOD FINAL NOTE PAD
XYZ 1/9BM
TOL1/20DH
BA1/30AF
AMZN2/2DH
XLNX2/6AF
DER3/3BM
TEAM3/6DH
HAND WRITTEN BY CHRONOLOGICAL ORDER BY EARNINGS RELEASE
DIGITAL MONTH WITH TRADING DAY TIME ALPHA CHARACTER,
DIGITAL DAY OF MONTH STOCK SYMBOL, ALPHA CHARCTER DAY
OF WEEK EARNINGS RELEASE

CHAPTER 8

STOCK INVESTING GAME PLAN SELL AFTER EARNINGS REPORT A STOCK TRADING METHOD PURCHASE STOCKS

When To Purchase A Stock With Stock Investing Game Plan Sell After Earnings Report A Stock Trading Method
To purchase stocks for a Stock Investing Game Plan Sell After Earnings Report a stock trading method is a very simple and basic activity. With Stock Investing Game Plan Sell After Earnings Report trading method a stock to purchase a stock, you complete your broker stock purchase transaction 3 to 4 or additional trading days prior to each stock earnings release date. In most situations, this stock purchase window allows a stock market price to rise and on an earnings release day to have a stock market price increase above your purchase price with a profit matches your investment goals. After a stock market price increase matches or exceeds your investment goal, for a profit you sell your stock through a broker.

   A company (symbol) earnings date information is obtain from one of the following (free on the internet) financial company reports is listed on your Final Note Pad. These are
(1) Zacks Earnings Calendar, Earnings Report or Stock
     Overview,
(2) Yahoo Earnings Calendar and Finance,
(3) GOOGL/NASDAQ/ZACKs Earnings report,
(4) Broker such as Schwab Company Research Page,
(5) Bloomberg Calendar of Earnings and
(6) your past Work Sheets.

Use A Stock Price Chart To Determine A Stock Purchase Window Day Number Before Earnings Report
When an investor uses the Stock Investing Game Plan Sell After Earnings Report a stock trading method, a very important activity is to determine a stock quality. We have reviewed several means to determine a stock as a quality stock for the Stock Investing Game Plan Sell After Earnings Report a stock trading method.

   When to complete a stock purchase before a stock's earnings release day information provides an investor with minimum day number for funds to be allocated for a stock purchase until a stock's earnings release. In general a 3 to 4 day or up to 5 day window is acceptable. To confirm this 3 to 4 day stock purchase window or add 1 or 2 days to a stock 3 to 4 day purchase window, an investor reviews a stock's previous quarter or two quarters market price movement chart that shows a stock's market price movement before a stock's previous quarter earnings release day. With this information and knowing history repeats, an investor determines a stock purchase window day number before a stock's earnings release. We refer a reader to (Exhibit 8 – 1). This example shows EL stock market price movement and day number prior to EL earnings release day. For additional stock market price movement charts we refer a reader to the charts at the chapter end (Exhibit 8 - 1 to Exhibit 8 - 36).

EXHIBIT 8 - 1

ESTEE LAUDER COMPANIES (EL)

STOCK INVESTING GAME PLAN SELLING AFTER EARNINGS REPORT A
STOCK TRADING METHOD STOCK PRICE MOVEMENT

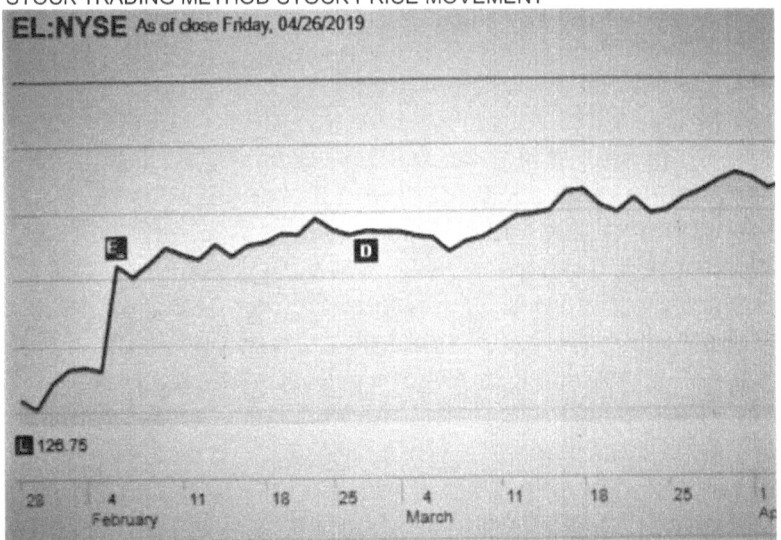

From Charles Schwab
E = EARNINGS ANNOUNCEMENT

SYMBOL	DATE	TRADE	DOLLARS
EL	2/1	PURCHASE	$132.53
	2/5	SELL	$150.01
		PER SHARE PROFIT	$12.48

300 SHARE PROFIT x $12.48 = $3,744 - $10.00 = $3,734
Broker Fee & Exchange Commission = $10.00

How to Obtain A Stock Market Purchase Price For Stock Investing Game Plan Sell After Earnings Report A Stock Trading Method A Stock Investing Game Plan Sell After Earnings Report a stock trading method stock purchase market price component is one of the two price factors that determine your Stock Investing Game Plan Sell After Earnings Report trading method stock trading profit.   Your knowledge of a stock most recent market price establishes your stock purchase price. Your stock trading profit is based on your stock investment goals and difference between your broker stock market purchase price and broker sell price. Your investment goals of a flat profit or percent return on an investment are what motivate you to invest (purchase stocks) and difference between your broker stock purchase market price and stock sell price exceeds your investment goal triggers your stock sell trade transaction.

    During a stock trading day to obtain a stock recent market purchase price, you access your stock broker program or cell phone app trade section or obtain a stock market price or from a TV business program such as CNBC stock symbol ticker price or news alert.   These are

(1) Broker Program

Your broker program or cell phone app trade program section is a very important key to completing a broker stock trade purchase. After accessing your broker account program trade section, the section shows you a stock symbol, most recent stock market price, bid price and ask price. This provides you with a stock recent market purchase price range for your stock purchase transaction through your stock broker. By using your stock broker trade program your ability to complete a stock purchase transaction is very quick due to your presently on your stock broker trade page and

(2) CNBC TV Ticker Tape

Another method to obtain a stock recent market price source has you obtain current prices from a TV business program such as CNBC stock symbol ticker price or news alert. On a CNBC TV screen stock symbols and most recent stock market prices are streaming along the screen bottom. If a stock symbol and stock market price has a red color, then a stock recent market price had a decrease from a stock previous market price.   If a stock symbol and stock market price has a green color, then a stock recent market price had an increase from a stock previous stock market price.   If a stock symbol and stock recent market price has a white color, then a stock market price had a no movement from a stock previous stock market price.

Stock Investing Game Plan Sell After Earnings Report A Stock Trading Method Work Sheet Used To Project Your Potential Stock Purchases

Stock Investing Game Plan Sell After Earnings Report A Stock Trading Method Work Sheet can be used to help schedule your stock purchases. On a Work Sheet you have identified a month earnings release day and your anticipated stock purchase day. With the unique Work Sheet identification and qualified stock information and recent stock market stock price you can project each earnings release anticipated funds to purchase each qualified stock.

To use a Work Sheet as a tool to project your Stock Investing Game Plan Sell After Earnings Report A Stock Trading Method investment funds requires several entries. These basic Work Sheet entries are (1) each qualified stock earnings release day of week, (2) your proposed stock share purchase quantity and (3) your stock preferred purchase price.

To determine your required investment funds for each earnings release week of a month or day of week, you complete several additional steps. From your broker program or CNBC TV you obtain a recent stock market stock price. This stock price you enter under the Work Sheet purchase column and is your stock potential purchase price. Your computer completes two calculations. These are (1) an earnings release day stock quantity purchase price (share number times stock price) and (2) total required funds to purchase all stocks (quantity) for each earnings release day of a week. See Exhibit 8- 2)

As you enter a stock new purchase price, for each stock and earnings release day of a week, on your Work Sheet your computer completes (updates) your required Stock Investing Game Plan Sell After Earnings Report A Stock Trading Method investment funds to complete your stock purchase (s). After your stock market stock price reaches your stock preferred or profitable price, you have your broker complete a stock purchase. For stock final Work Sheet purchase price entry, enter your stock broker stock purchase cost and broker stock sell commission and exchange fees.

How Does A Stock's Market Price Influence Your Stock Purchase As an investor starts stock trading with a Stock Investing Game Plan Sell After Earnings Report a stock trading method, a key stock purchase consideration is the stock purchase quantity or share number. This consideration is a complex issue due to an investor's stock quantity purchase is directed by available investment funds, market stock price and investor ability to take a financial risk.

EXHIBIT 8 - 2

STOCK INVESTING GAME PLAN SELL AFTER EARNINGS REPORT STOCK TRADING METHOD PURCHASE STOCK PRICE WORK SHEET

1/5 DIGITAL PURCHASE DAY OF MONTH
1/9 DIGITAL EARNINGS RELEASE DAY OF MONTH

(1) DIGITAL ALPHA MTH & DAY TIME	(2) DAY DATE	(3) STK SYML	(4) ANALYST RANK (1)	(5) (2)	(6) PCHAS NBER #	(7) STK B-EN $	(8) STK GN/LS $	(9) STK GN LS %	(10) PORT VLE $
1/9BM	MON	XYZ	3	**	300	75.21			$22,563
1/20DH	TUES	TOL	2	*	300	66.09			$19,827
1/30AF	WEDS	BA	1	**	300	23,66			$7,098
2/2DH	MON	AMZN	1	**	200	76.00			$22,800
2/2AF	MON	SPLK	1	**	300				
2/6AF	FRI	XLNX	2	**	300				
3/3BM	THUR	DER	3	*	300				
3/6DH	THUR	TEAM	2	**	300				

(7) Your enter common stock break-even dollar PURCHASE value .
After your broker purchase the stock you revise the stock break even price and portfolio value

An investor's available investment funds consideration options are basically (1) $25,000 and (2) $100,000 or more.
The first is $25,000 or limited available investment funds. With the limited investment funds an investor is restricted to purchase a total share quantity that does not exceed the $25,000. An investor purchase share quantity is determined by a stock recent market price.   The three basic stock market prices are (1) high price

stock has a price range from $500 or above dollars, usually the stock is considered an industry sector leader, a stock has an excellent earnings record and usually the stocks in the group have a minimal risk for a poor earnings release and large financial companies (pension and hedge funds) have a tendency to desire these high priced stocks in their portfolio which with good earnings release and a potential for an increase in a stock price, (2) medium price stock has a price range from $150 to $500 dollars, usually the company is considered an industry sector leader, a stock has an excellent earnings record and company stocks in the group have a minimal risk for a poor earnings release and large financial companies (pension and hedge funds) have a tendency to desire these stocks in their portfolio which with good earnings release and potential for increase in a stock price and (3) low price stock has a price range from $25.00 to $100 dollars, a young company, not an industry leader, does not have a earnings record and stock market price direction could be an increase or decrease to a stock price.

   With a $25,000 available investment funds and a high price stock with a market price that exceeds $500.00 or more dollars ($) (example GOOGL with stock market price of $1,888), an investor has an opportunity to purchase 13 shares for $24,554. In most cases, there is some risk for a poor earnings release. The stock purchase cost includes $10.00 for broker commissions and exchange fees. If GOOGL has a good earnings release and the market stock price increases by $60.00 per share, an investor earns a $780 profit or 3.6% return.   If an investor has $100,000 or more dollars available to invest, then for the above mentioned example, an investor would purchase additional shares and the $ profit were increase by a share quantity with the same % return.

     With a $25,000 available investment funds and a medium price stock with a market price that exceeds $100.00 to $500.00 (example Face Book with a market price of $190.55), an investor has an opportunity to purchase 131 shares for $24,972. In most cases, there is minimal risk for a poor earnings release. The stock purchase cost includes $10.00 for broker commissions and exchange fees. If Face Book has a good earnings release and a market stock price increases by $15.25 per share, an investor earns a $1,997.75 profit or 8.0% return.

If an investor has $100,000 or more dollars available to invest, then for the above mentioned example, an investor would purchase additional shares and the $ profit were increase by a share quantity with the same % return.

With a $25,000 available investment funds and a medium price stock with a market price that is approximately $25.00 to $100.00 (example is Rent A Center) that has a market price of $24.25), the investor has an opportunity to purchase 1030 shares for $24,988. In most cases, there is some risk for a poor earnings release. In most cases, there is some risk for a poor earnings release. The stock purchase cost includes $10.00 for broker commissions and exchange fees. If Face Book has a good earnings release and the market stock price increases by $1.25 per share, the investor earns a $1,287.50 profit or 5.1% return.

If an investor has $100,000 or more dollars available to invest, then for the above mentioned example, the investor would purchase additional shares and the $ profit were increase by a share quantity with the same % return.

When we compare the three stock price categories, the conclusions are (1) investment sums understood as to which would have the largest share number purchased, (2) high and medium price stocks have lower risks than low price stocks and (3) medium price stocks have a greater dollar return than a high price and low price stocks.

Different Corporation Stocks Purchase For Stock Investing Game Plan Sell After Earnings Report A Stock Trading Method
A Stock Investing Game Plan Sell After Earnings Report a stock trading method factor is your single or different company stocks your purchase for an earnings release day of a month. A stock purchased plan is based on these factors
(1) One Company Stock
With one company stock for a Stock Investing Game Plan Sell After Earnings Report a stock trading method stock purchase plan, your stock research has provided only one qualified company stock to be purchased for an earnings release day of a month. One company stock to be purchased features are (a) easy to complete your stock Work Sheet purchase price notation and stock Computer Spread

Screen Sheet purchase price notation and (b) easier to allocate your next earnings release trading day investment money to one stock or

(2) Multiple Or Different Company Stocks
With a multiple or different company stock shares stock purchase plan means your stock research provided multiple qualified company stocks to be purchased for an earnings release day of a month. The multiple or different company stock purchase plan features are (a) assure accurate company stock purchase price notation on your stock Work Sheet and stock Computer Spread Sheet, (b) with a different company stocks for one earnings release day of month there is potential for different purchase market prices which is more difficult to allocate limited investment funds and (c) for a high priced stock your able to purchase a smaller stock share quantity.

Stock Purchase With Same Share Quantity From Different Corporations For Stock Investing Game Plan Sell After Earnings Report A Stock Trading Method
A Stock Investing Game Plan Sell After Earnings Report a stock trading method factor has you purchase your company stocks with different share quantities for an earnings release day of a month. Company stocks with different share quantity purchase plan is based on these factors

(1) One Standard Stock Share Quantity
With one standard stock share quantity for each Stock Investing Game Plan Sell After Earnings Report a stock trading method stock purchase has you purchase one stock share quantity for each different company purchase stock trade transaction. With a standard stock share quantity per purchase plan, the features are (a) easy to complete your stock Work Sheet purchase quantity notation and stock Computer Spread Screen Sheet purchase quantity notation,
(b) a high market price stock has a higher purchase cost with fewer shares and (c) difficult to allocated your investment funds for one earnings release day of a month for stock purchases or

(2) Multiple Or Different Stock Share Quantity
With multiple stock purchase share quantity for each earnings release day of month stock trading purchase, your purchase standard quantity of stock share quantity varies per each different

company stock.   The flexible approach features are (a) requires accurate stock share quantity notation on your stock Work Sheet and stock Computer Spread Sheet, (b) more difficult to allocate your trading day available investment money and (c) for a high priced common stock your able to purchase a stock share quantity.

Given investment money flexibility, stock market price and ability to take a risk, you are able to vary your stock purchase share quantity and company share quantity purchase.

Stock Purchase Price End Digit For Stock Investing Game Plan Sell After Earnings Report A Stock Trading Method

Another Stock Investing Game Plan Sell After Earnings Report a stock trading method situation is a stock purchase market price that you send to your broker with your stock dollar purchase amount. The two stock market price purchase amounts are a broker stock purchase trade transaction price that has a price with a last price digit odd number such as 1, 3, 5, 7 or 9.   Stock purchase trade transactions that end with an odd digit last number (Examples are $305 or $301.01). When there is stock wide market piece movement, a broker stock purchase trade transaction that ends with an even digit number such as 0, 2, 4, 6, & 8, then there is greater potential not to be completed due to the fact that most retail stock investors use stock purchase trade transaction dollar number that ends with an even digit such as $300 or $406.88.

Stock Purchase Price Plus Broker Commission & Exchange Fee

For each broker stock purchase, your stock purchase price includes a stock market price, plus a stock broker's flat commission $ (estimated $5 to purchase and $5 to sell). When you sell a stock, your broker has to charge a sell exchange fee. A sell exchange fee is percent value that is deducted from your cash received from a broker stock sell transaction. On your stock Work Sheet and Computer Spread Sheet, your break-even stock purchase dollar value is a round trip stock broker flat commission purchase fee (estimated $11) and sell transaction exchange fee. If your stock purchase was 300 shares then your on-line broker flat commission and exchange fee allowance for 300 shares = $11/300 = $.04 or for 400 shares = $11/400 = $.03.

If your stock purchase was for 300 stock shares at $93 per share stock market price, then on your stock Work Sheet or stock Computer Spread Screen Sheet a stock break-even purchase price is $93.04.

EXHIBIT 8 – 3

APPLE (AAPL)

STOCK INVESTING GAME PLAN SELLING AFTER EARNINGS REPORT A STOCK TRADING METHOD STOCK PRICE MOVEMENT

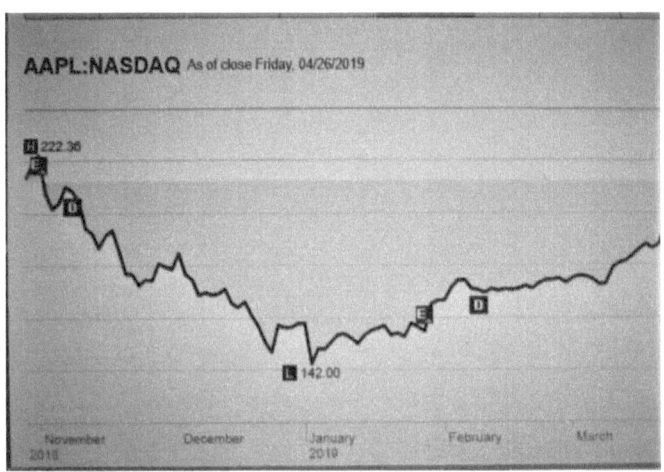

From Charles Schwab

E = EARNINGS ANNOUNCEMENT

SYMBOL	DATE	TRADE	DOLLARS
AAPL	1/27	PURCHASE	$157.05
	1/29	SELL	$159.12
		PER SHARE PROFIT	$2.07

300 SHARE PROFIT x $2.07 = $621 - $10.00 = $621.00
Broker Fee & Exchange Commission = $10.00

EXHIBIT 8 - 4

ACCENTURE PLC (ACN)

STOCK INVESTING GAME PLAN SELLING AFTER EARNINGS REPORT A
STOCK TRADING METHOD STOCK PRICE MOVEMENT

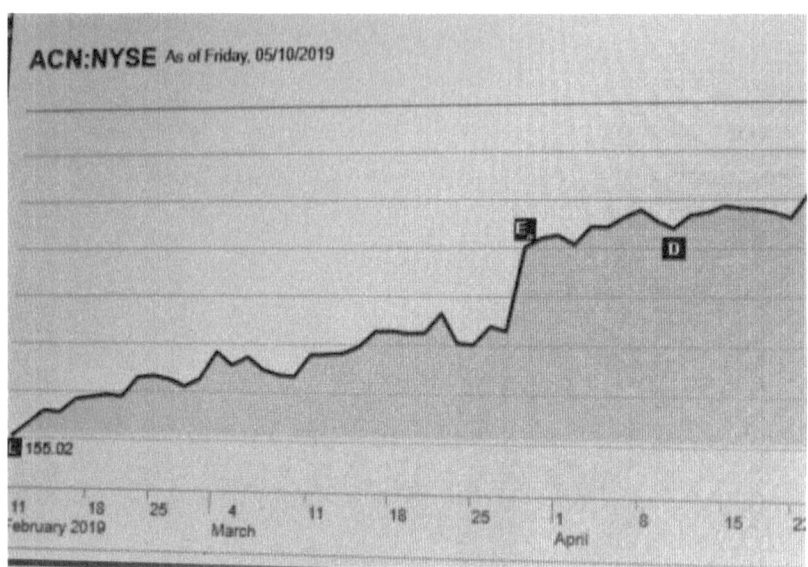

From Charles Schwab

E = EARNINGS ANNOUNCEMENT

SYMBOL	DATE	TRADE	DOLLARS
PLAY	3/14	PURCHASE	$164.75
	3/22	SELL	$166.51
	PER SHARE PROFIT		$1.76

300 SHARE PROFIT x $1.76 = $528 - $10.00 = $518
Broker Fee & Exchange Commission = $10.00

EXHIBIT 8 - 5

AMAZON (AMZN)

STOCK INVESTING GAME PLAN SELLING AFTER EARNINGS REPORT A
STOCK TRADING METHOD STOCK PRICE MOVEMENT

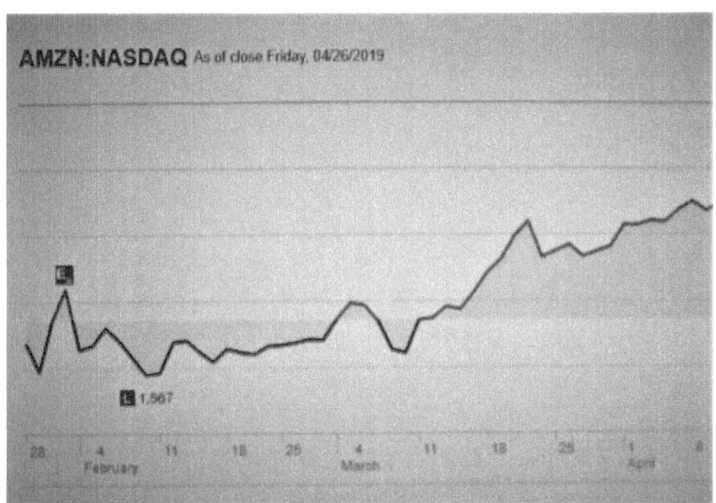

From Charles Schwab

E = EARNINGS ANNOUNCEMENT

SYMBOL	DATE	TRADE	DOLLARS
AMZN	12/6	PURCHASE	$1,701.00
	1/31	SELL	$1,730.00
	PER SHARE PROFIT		$29.00

300 SHARE PROFIT x $29.00 = $8,700 - $10.00 = $ 8,690

Broker Fee & Exchange Commission = $10.00

EXHIBIT 8 – 6

AMEDISYS INC. (AMED)

STOCK INVESTING GAME PLAN SELLING AFTER EARNINGS REPORT A
STOCK TRADING METHOD STOCK PRICE MOVEMENT

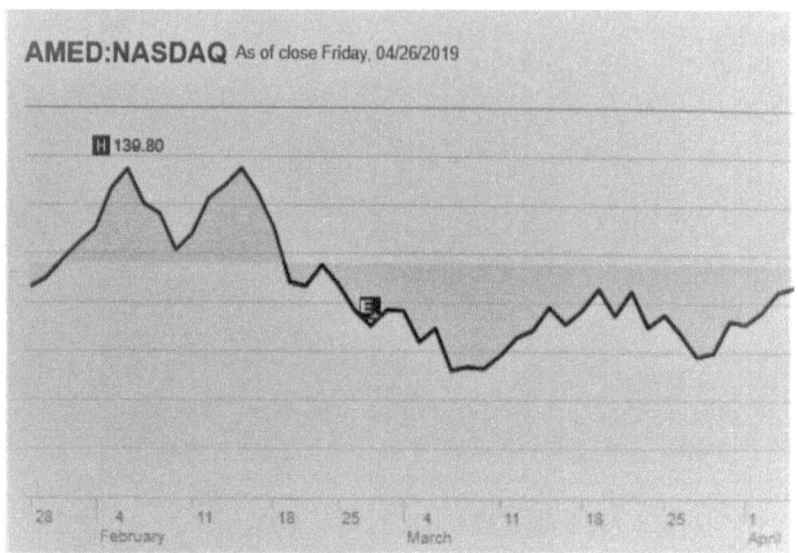

From Charles Schwab

E = EARNINGS ANNOUNCEMENT

SYMBOL	DATE	TRADE	DOLLARS
AMED	2/27	PURCHASE	$48.97
	3/1	SELL	$52.18
		PER SHARE PROFI	$ 3.21

300 SHARE PROFIT x $3.21 = $963 - $10.00 = $953.00
Broker Fee & Exchange Commission = $10.00

EXHIBIT 8 - 7

AUTO ZONE (AZO)

STOCK INVESTING GAME PLAN SELLING AFTER EARNINGS REPORT A
STOCK TRADING METHOD STOCK PRICE MOVEMENT

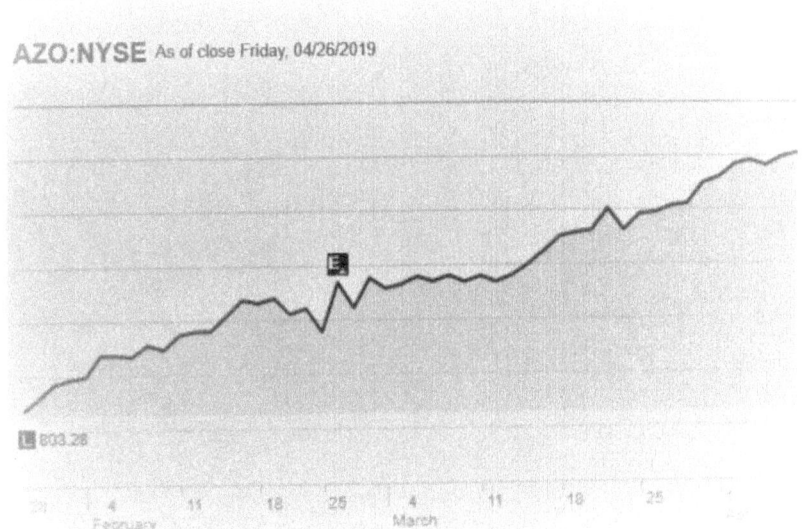

From Charles Schwab

E = EARNINGS ANNOUNCEMENT

SYMBOL	DATE	TRADE	DOLLARS
AZO	2/14	PURCHAS	$1,080.00
	2/26	SELL	$1,138.32
		PER SHARE PROFIT	$58.32

300 SHARE PROFIT x $58.32 = $17,496 - $10.00 = $17,486
Broker Fee & Exchange Commission = $10.00

EXHIBIT 8 - 8

BROADCOM INC. (AVGO)

STOCK INVESTING GAME PLAN SELLING AFTER EARNINGS REPORT A
STOCK TRADING METHOD STOCK PRICE MOVEMENT

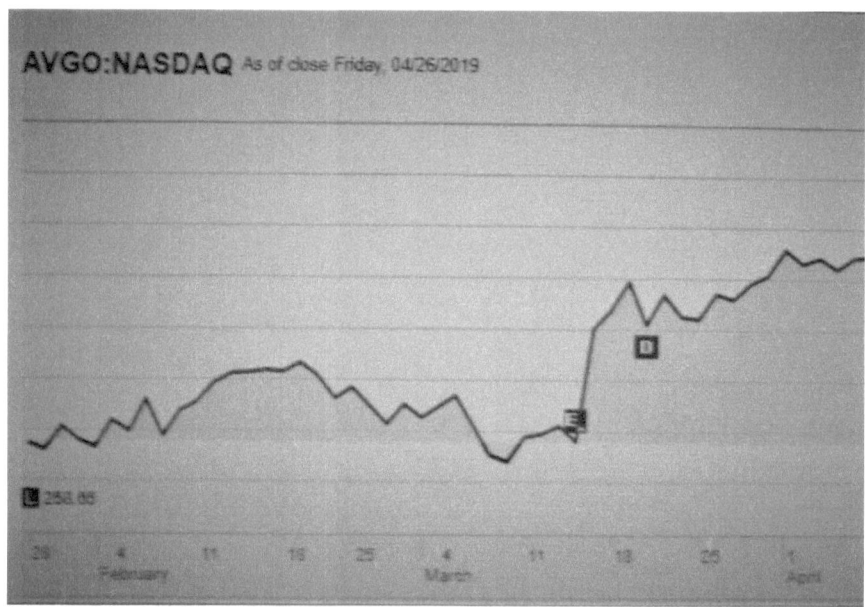

From Charles Schwab

E = EARNINGS ANNOUNCEMENT

SYMBOL	DATE	TRADE	DOLLARS
AVGO	3/8	PURCHASE	$262.59
	3/11	SELL	$268.31
		PER SHARE PROFIT	$6.58

300 SHARE PROFIT x $5.72 = $1,716 - $10.00 = $1,704.00
Broker Fee & Exchange Commission = $10.00

EXHIBIT 8 - 9

SALES FORCE (CRM)

STOCK INVESTING GAME PLAN SELLING AFTER EARNINGS REPORT A
STOCK TRADING METHOD STOCK PRICE MOVEMENT

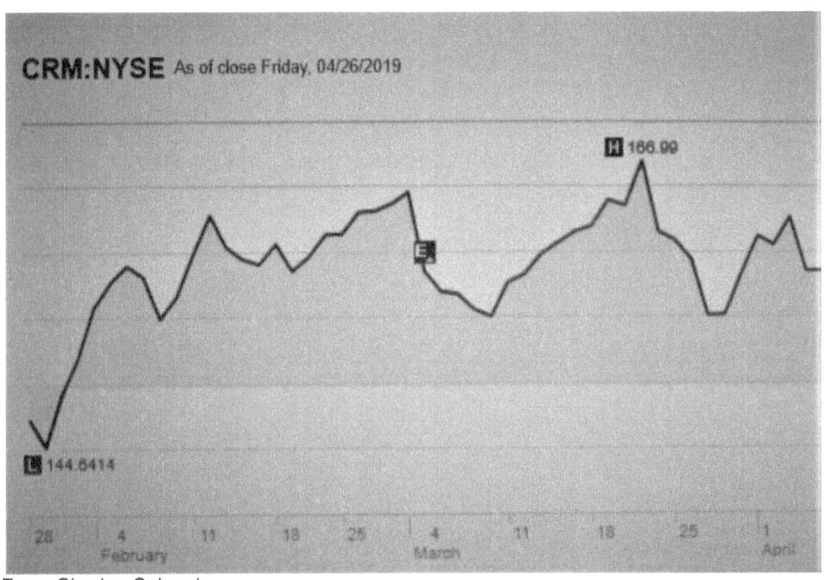

From Charles Schwab

E = EARNINGS ANNOUNCEMENT

SYMBOL	DATE	TRADE	DOLLARS
CRM	11/21	PURCHASE	$124.79
	11/27	SELL	$132.06
		PER SHARE PROFIT	-$7.27

300 SHARE PROFIT x $-7.27 = $-2,181 - $10.00 = -$2,171.00
Broker Fee & Exchange Commission = $10.00

EXHIBIT 8 - 10

THE COOPER COMPANIES (COO)

STOCK INVESTING GAME PLAN SELLING AFTER EARNINGS REPORT A
STOCK TRADING METHOD STOCK PRICE MOVEMENT

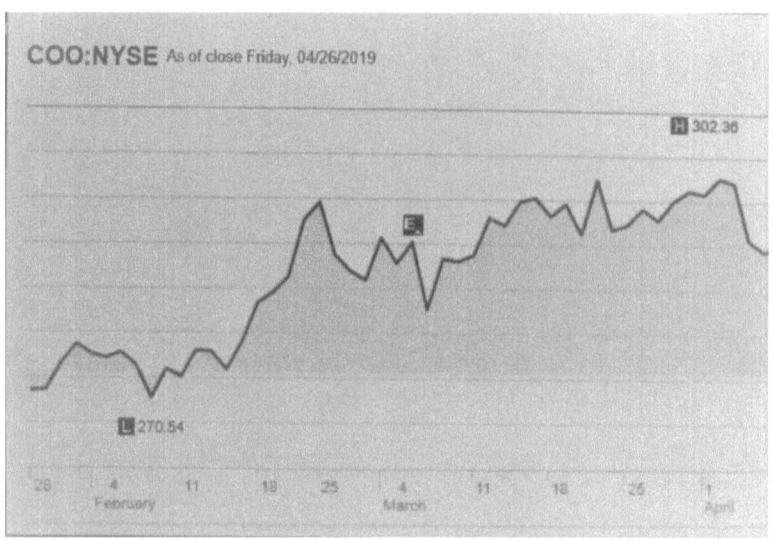

From Charles Schwab
E = EARNINGS ANNOUNCEMENT

SYMBOL	DATE	TRADE	DOLLARS
COO	3/1	PURCHASE	$291.23
	3/5	SELL	$294.17
	PER SHARE PROFIT		$ 2.94

300 SHARE PROFIT x $2.94 = $882 - $10.00 = $872.00
Broker Fee & Exchange Commission = $10.00

EXHIBIT 8 - 11

COST CO (COST)

STOCK INVESTING GAME PLAN SELLING AFTER EARNINGS REPORT A
STOCK TRADING METHOD STOCK PRICE MOVEMENT

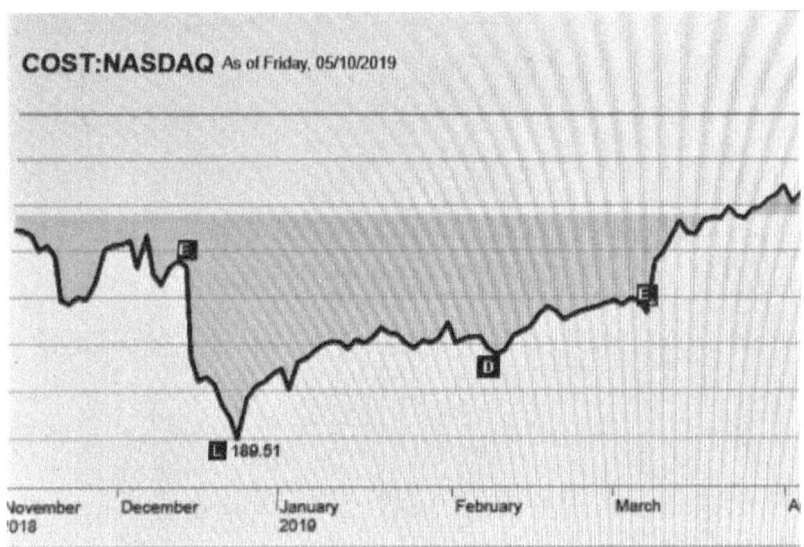

COST:NASDAQ As of Friday, 05/10/2019

189.51

November   December   January   February   March   A
2018   2019

From Charles Schwab

E = EARNINGS ANNOUNCEMENT

SYMBOL	DATE	TRADE	DOLLARS
COST	3/4	PURCHASE	$220.56
	3/8	SELL	$226.00
		PER SHARE PROFIT	$5.44

300 SHARE PROFIT x $5.44 = $1,632 - $10.00 = $1,622
Broker Fee & Exchange Commission = $10.00

EXHIBIT 8 - 12

DOLLAR TREE (DLTR)

STOCK INVESTING GAME PLAN SELLING AFTER EARNINGS REPORT A
STOCK TRADING METHOD STOCK PRICE MOVEMENT

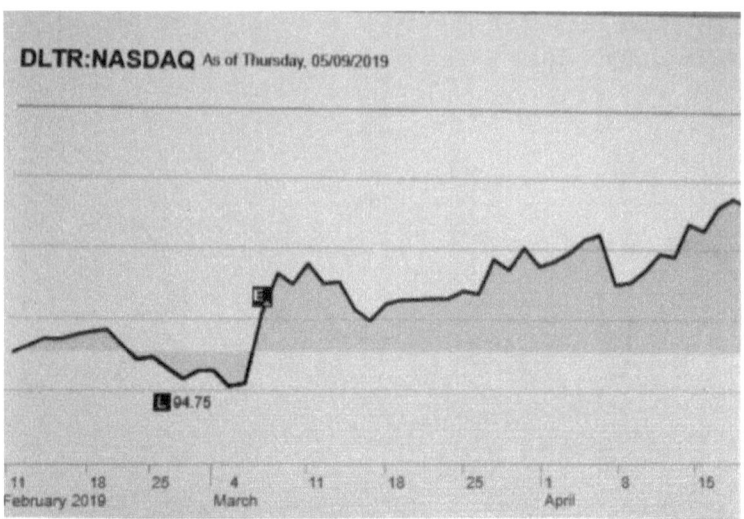

DLTR:NASDAQ As of Thursday, 05/09/2019

94.75

| 11 | 18 | 25 | 4 | 11 | 18 | 25 | 1 | 8 | 15 |
February 2019 March April

From Charles Schwab

E = EARNINGS ANNOUNCEMENT

SYMBOL	DATE	TRADE	DOLLARS
DLTR	3/1	PURCHASE	$97.13
	3/6	SELL	$99.07
	PER SHARE PROFIT		$ 1.94

300 SHARE PROFIT x $1.94 = $582 - $10.00 = $572.00
Broker Fee & Exchange Commission = $10.00

EXHIBIT 8 - 13

ESTEE LAUDER COMPANIES (EL)

STOCK INVESTING GAME PLAN SELLING AFTER EARNINGS REPORT A
STOCK TRADING METHOD STOCK PRICE MOVEMENT

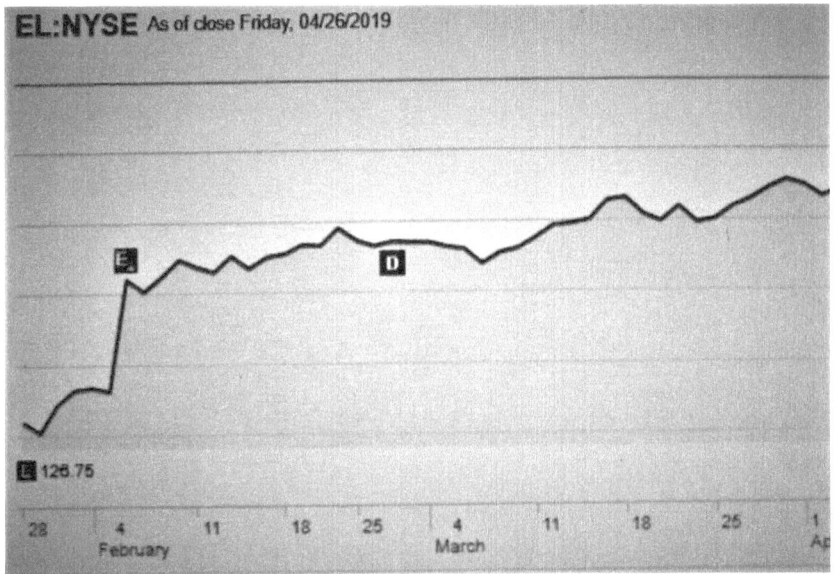

From Charles Schwab

E = EARNINGS ANNOUNCEMENT

SYMBOL	DATE	TRADE	DOLLARS
EL	2/1	PURCHASE	$132.53
	2/5	SELL	$150.01
		PER SHARE PROFIT	$12.48

300 SHARE PROFIT x $12.48 = $3,744 - $10.00 = $3,734
Broker Fee & Exchange Commission = $10.00

EXHIBIT 8 - 14

FIVE (FIVE)

STOCK INVESTING GAME PLAN SELLING AFTER EARNINGS REPORT A
STOCK TRADING METHOD STOCK PRICE MOVEMENT

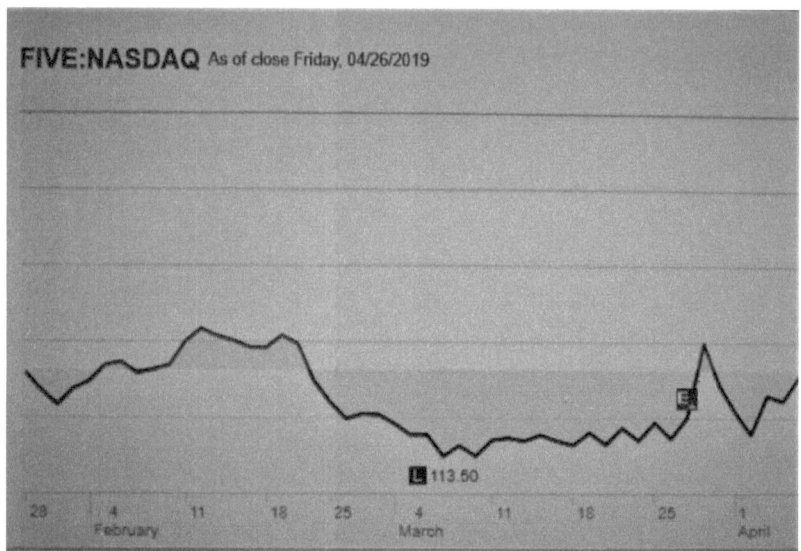

From Charles Schwab

E = EARNINGS ANNOUNCEMENT

SYMBOL	DATE	TRADE	DOLLARS
FIVE	3/12	PURCHASE	$115.61
	3/27	SELL	$123.09
		PER SHARE PROFIT	$7.48

300 SHARE PROFIT x $7.48 = $2,244 - $10.00 = $2,234
Broker Fee & Exchange Commission = $10.00

EXHIBIT 8 - 15

FOOT LOCKER (FL)

STOCK INVESTING GAME PLAN SELLING AFTER EARNINGS REPORT A
STOCK TRADING METHOD STOCK PRICE MOVEMENT

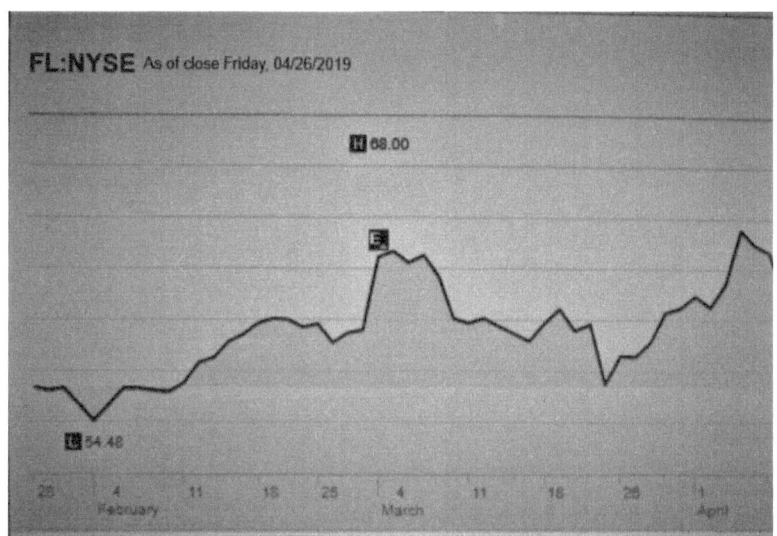

From Charles Schwab

E = EARNINGS ANNOUNCEMENT

SYMBOL	DATE	TRADE	DOLLARS
FL	2/27	PURCHASE	$58.89
	3/1	SELL	$67.24
		PER SHARE PROFIT	$ 8.35

300 SHARE PROFIT x $8.35 = $2,505 - $10.00 = $2,495.00
Broker Fee & Exchange Commission = $10.00

EXHIBIT 8 - 16

GENERAL MOTORS (GM)

STOCK INVESTING GAME PLAN SELLING AFTER EARNINGS REPORT A
STOCK TRADING METHOD STOCK PRICE MOVEMENT

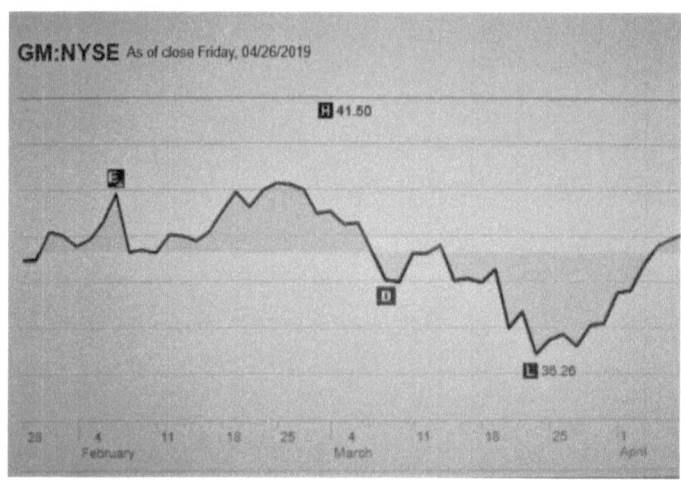

From Charles Schwab

E = EARNINGS ANNOUNCEMENT

SYMBOL	DATE	TRADE	DOLLARS
GM	2/4	PURCHASE	$38.97
	2/6	SELL	$39.59
	PER SHARE PROFIT		$ .62

300 SHARE PROFIT x $.62 = $186 - $10.00 = $176.00
Broker Fee & Exchange Commission = $10.00

EXHIBIT 8 -17

GOOGL (GOOGL)

STOCK INVESTING GAME PLAN SELLING AFTER EARNINGS REPORT A
STOCK TRADING METHOD STOCK PRICE MOVEMENT

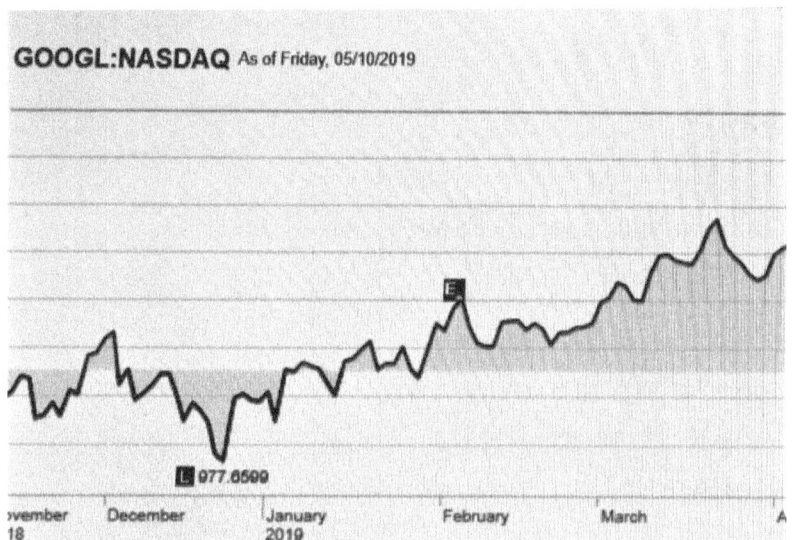

From Charles Schwab

E = EARNINGS ANNOUNCEMENT

SYMBOL	DATE	TRADE	DOLLARS
GOOGL	1/30	PURCHASE	$1,080.00
	2/4	SELL	$1,138.32
		PER SHARE PROFIT	$58.32

300 SHARE PROFIT x $58.32 = $17,496 - $10.00 = $17,486
Broker Fee & Exchange Commission = $10.00

EXHIBIT 8 - 18

GUIDE WIRE SOLUTIONS INC. (GWRE)

STOCK INVESTING GAME PLAN SELLING AFTER EARNINGS REPORT A
STOCK TRADING METHOD STOCK PRICE MOVEMENT

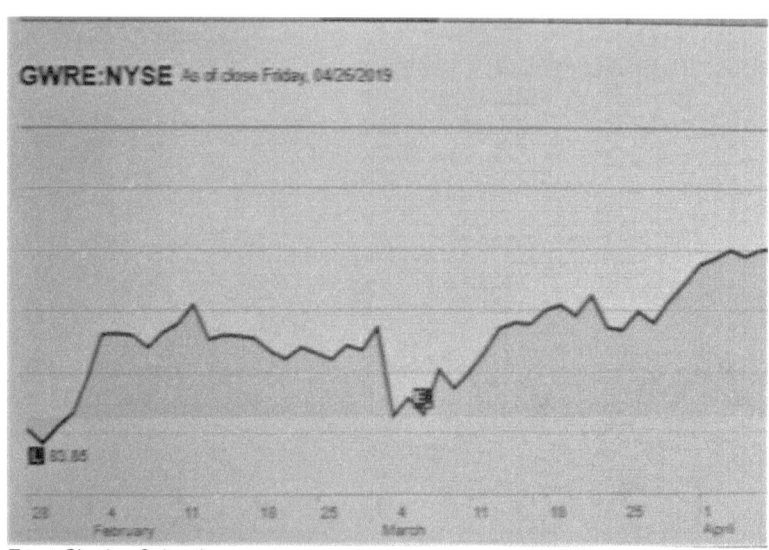

From Charles Schwab

E = EARNINGS ANNOUNCEMENT

SYMBOL	DATE	TRADE	DOLLARS
GWRE	2/28	PURCHASE	$92.01
	3/7	SELL	$93.12
		PER SHARE PROFIT	$1.11

300 SHARE PROFIT x $1.11 = $333 - $10.00 = $323.00
Broker Fee & Exchange Commission = $10.00

EXHIBIT 8 -19

INTERNATIONAL BUSINSS MACHINES (IBM)

STOCK INVESTING GAME PLAN SELLING AFTER EARNINGS REPORT A
STOCK TRADING METHOD STOCK PRICE MOVEMENT

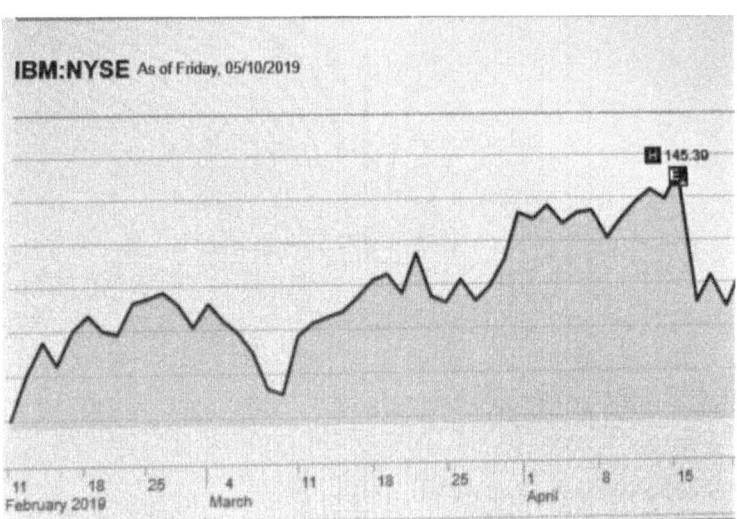

From Charles Schwab

E = EARNINGS ANNOUNCEMENT

SYMBOL	DATE	TRADE	DOLLARS
IBM	4/11	PURCHASE	$120.80
	4/16	SELL	$122.89
		PER SHARE PROFIT	$ 2.09

300 SHARE PROFIT x $2.09 = $627 - $10.00 = $626.00
Broker Fee & Exchange Commission = $10.00

EXHIBIT 8 - 20

INNOVATIVE INDUSTRIAL PROPERTIES (IIPR)

STOCK INVESTING GAME PLAN SELLING AFTER EARNINGS REPORT A
STOCK TRADING METHOD STOCK PRICE MOVEMENT

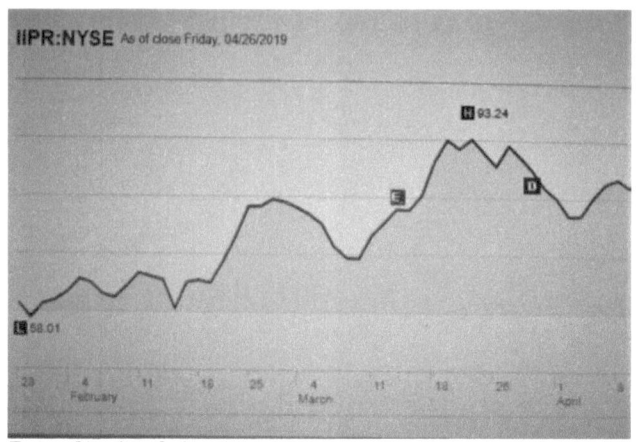

From Charles Schwab
E = EARNINGS ANNOUNCEMENT

SYMBOL	DATE	TRADE	DOLLARS
IIPR	3/12	PURCHASE	$27.25
	3/13	SELL	$80.37
	PER SHARE PROFIT		$3.12

300 SHARE PROFIT x $3.12 = $936 - $10.00 = $926.00
Broker Fee & Exchange Commission = $10.00

EXHIBIT 8- 21

JABIL (JBL)

STOCK INVESTING GAME PLAN SELLING AFTER EARNINGS REPORT A
STOCK TRADING METHOD STOCK PRICE MOVEMENT

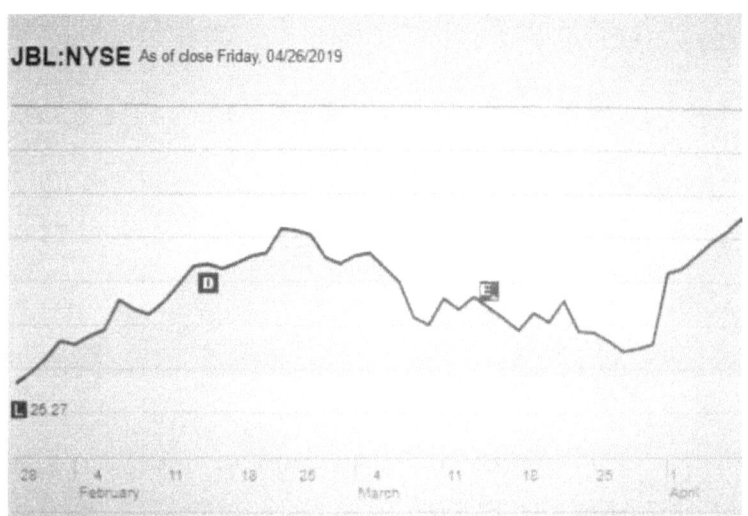

From Charles Schwab

E = EARNINGS ANNOUNCEMENT

SYMBOL	DATE	TRADE	DOLLARS
JBL	3/12	PURCHASE	$27.54
	3/13	SELL	$27.73
		PER SHARE PROFIT	$.19

300 SHARE PROFIT x $.19 = $57 - $10.00 = $56.00
Broker Fee & Exchange Commission = $10.00

EXHIBIT 8 - 22

MASTER CARD (MA)

STOCK INVESTING GAME PLAN SELLING AFTER EARNINGS REPORT A
STOCK TRADING METHOD STOCK PRICE MOVEMENT

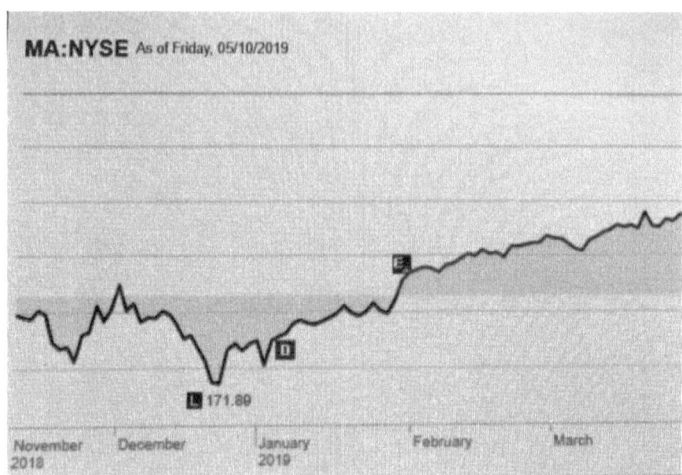

From Charles Schwab

E = EARNINGS ANNOUNCEMENT

SYMBOL	DATE	TRADE	DOLLARS
MA	1/27	PURCHASE	$200.10
	2/1	SELL	$217.03
		PER SHARE PROFIT	$16.93

300 SHARE PROFIT 300 x $16.93 - $10.00 = $5069
Broker Fee & Exchange Commission = $10.00

EXHIBIT 8 - 23

MONGO DB INC. (MDB)

STOCK INVESTING GAME PLAN SELLING AFTER EARNINGS REPORT A
STOCK TRADING METHOD STOCK PRICE MOVEMENT

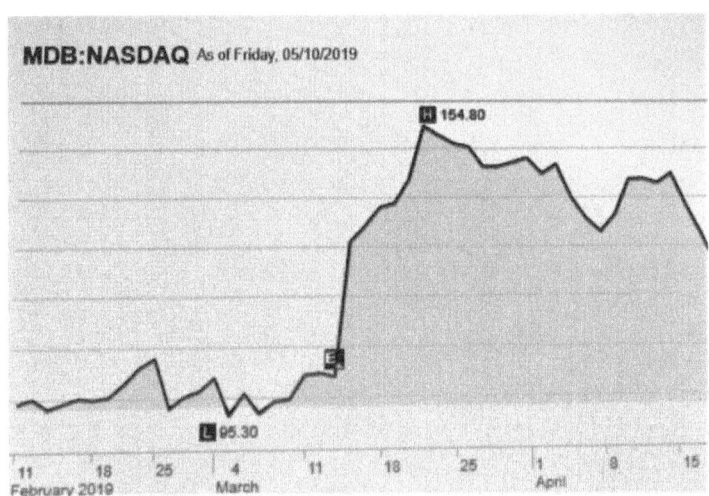

From Charles Schwab

E = EARNINGS ANNOUNCEMENT

SYMBOL	DATE	TRADE	DOLLARS
MDB	3/12	PURCHASE	$101.03
	3/15	SELL	$103.45
	PER SHARE PROFIT		$2.42

300 SHARE PROFIT x $2.42 = $726 - $10.00 = $716
Broker Fee & Exchange Commission = $10.00

EXHIBIT 8 - 24

MICROSOFT (MSFT)

STOCK INVESTING GAME PLAN SELLING AFTER EARNINGS REPORT A
STOCK TRADING METHOD STOCK PRICE MOVEMENT

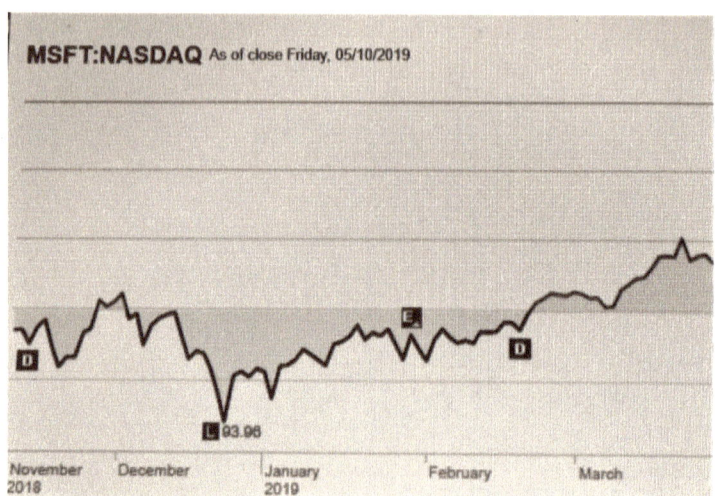

From Charles Schwab

E = EARNINGS ANNOUNCEMENT

SYMBOL	DATE	TRADE	DOLLARS
MSFT	1/11	PURCHASE	$103.11
	1/16	SELL	$115.27
	PER SHARE PROFIT		$ 12.16

300 SHARE PROFIT x $12.16 = $3,648 - $10.00 = $ 3,838.00
Broker Fee & Exchange Commission = $10.00

EXHIBIT 8 - 25

NETFLEX (NFLX)

STOCK INVESTING GAME PLAN SELLING AFTER EARNINGS REPORT A
STOCK TRADING METHOD STOCK PRICE MOVEMENT

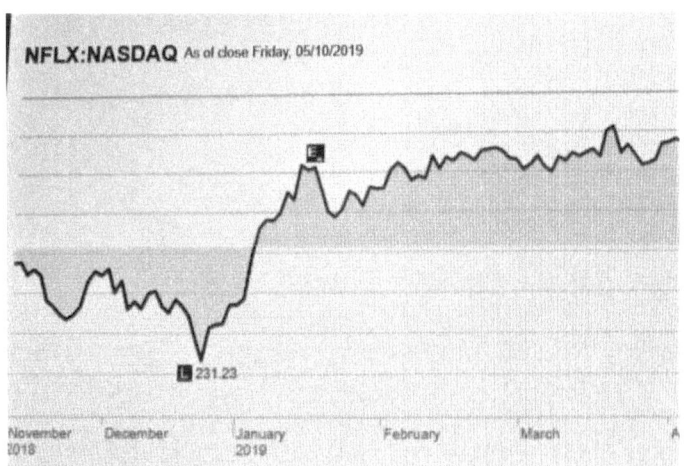

From Charles Schwab

E = EARNINGS ANNOUNCEMENT

SYMBOL	DATE	TRADE	DOLLARS
NFLX	1/11	PURCHASE	$322.16
	1/16	SELL	$351.75
		PER SHARE PROFIT	$ 29.59

300 SHARE PROFIT x $29.59 = $8,877 - $10.00 = $ 8,867.00
Broker Fee & Exchange Commission = $10.00

EXHIBIT 8 - 26

O'REILY AUTOMOTIVE INC. (ORLY)

STOCK INVESTING GAME PLAN SELLING AFTER EARNINGS REPORT A
STOCK TRADING METHOD STOCK PRICE MOVEMENT

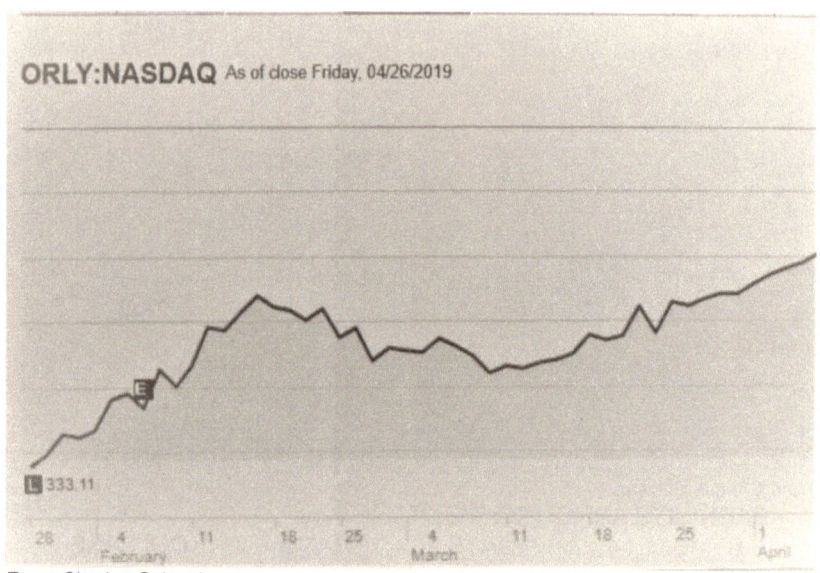

From Charles Schwab

E = EARNINGS ANNOUNCEMENT

SYMBOL	DATE	TRADE	DOLLARS
ORLY	2/4	PURCHASE	$349.00
	2/6	SELL	$366.00
		PER SHARE PROFIT	$ 17.00

300 SHARE PROFIT x $17.00 = $5,100 - $10.00 = $ 5.090
Broker Fee & Exchange Commission = $10.00

EXHIBIT 8 - 27

PALO ALTO NETWORKS INC. (PANW)

STOCK INVESTING GAME PLAN SELLING AFTER EARNINGS REPORT A
STOCK TRADING METHOD STOCK PRICE MOVEMENT

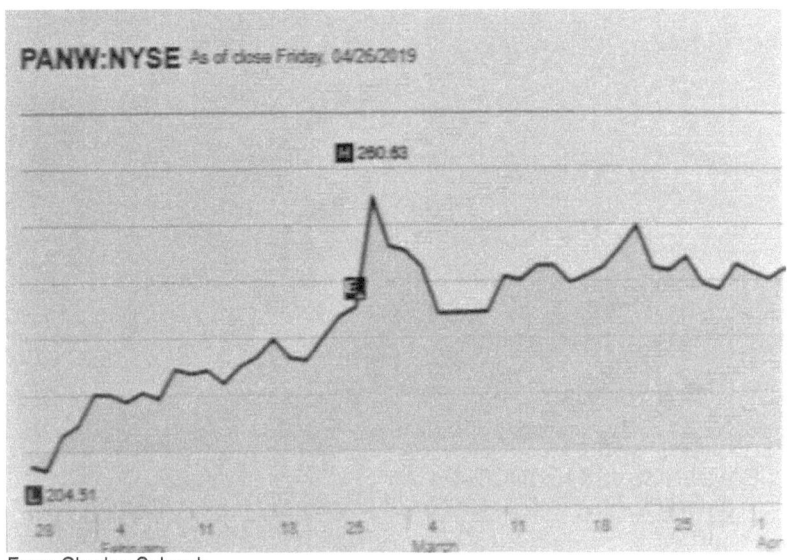

From Charles Schwab

E = EARNINGS ANNOUNCEMENT

SYMBOL	DATE	TRADE	DOLLARS
AZO	2/19	PURCHASE	$229.40
	2/26	SELL	$235.88
		PER SHARE PROFIT	$6.48

300 SHARE PROFIT x $6.48 = $1,944 - $10.00 = $ 1,944
Broker Fee & Exchange Commission = $10.00

EXHIBIT 8 - 28

DAVE & BUSTERS (PLAY)

STOCK INVESTING GAME PLAN SELLING AFTER EARNINGS REPORT A STOCK TRADING METHOD STOCK PRICE MOVEMENT

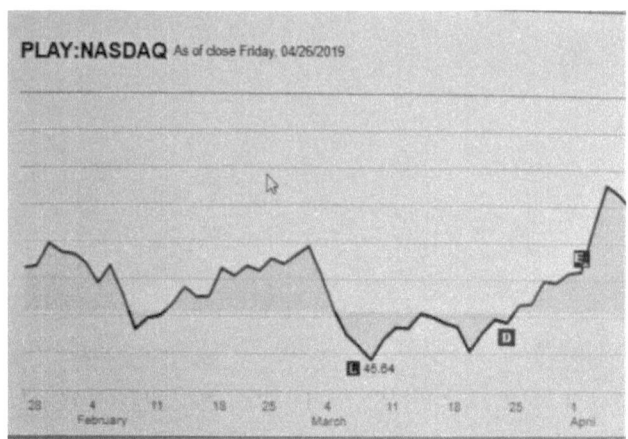

From Charles Schwab

E = EARNINGS ANNOUNCEMENT

SYMBOL	DATE	TRADE	DOLLARS
PLAY	3/27	PURCHASE	$48.92
	4/2	SELL	$49.71
		PER SHARE PROFIT	$.79

300 SHARE PROFIT x $.79 = $237 - $10.00 = $227
Broker Fee & Exchange Commission = $10.00

EXHIBIT 8 – 29

PRAH HEALTH SERVICES INC. (PRAH)

STOCK INVESTING GAME PLAN SELLING AFTER EARNINGS REPORT A
STOCK TRADING METHOD STOCK PRICE MOVEMENT

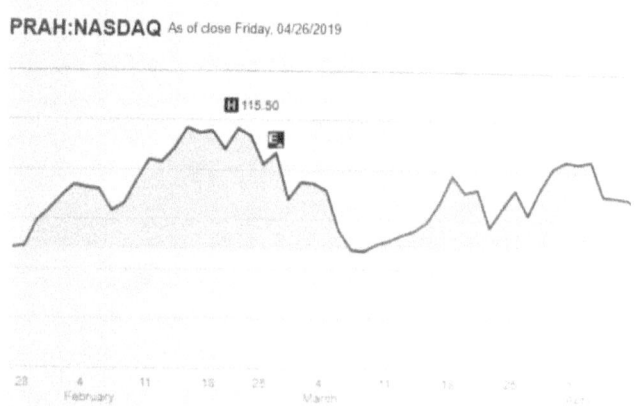

PRAH:NASDAQ As of close Friday, 04/26/2019

From Charles Schwab

E = EARNINGS ANNOUNCEMENT

SYMBOL	DATE	TRADE	DOLLARS
PRAH	2/22	PURCHASE	$112.55
	3/1	SELL	$-109.11
		PER SHARE PROFIT	$ - 3.44

300 SHARE PROFIT x -$3.44 = -$1,032 - $10.00 = -$1,022.00
Broker Fee & Exchange Commission = $10.00

EXHIBIT 8- 30

PVH CROP. (PVH)

STOCK INVESTING GAME PLAN SELLING AFTER EARNINGS REPORT A
STOCK TRADING METHOD STOCK PRICE MOVEMENT

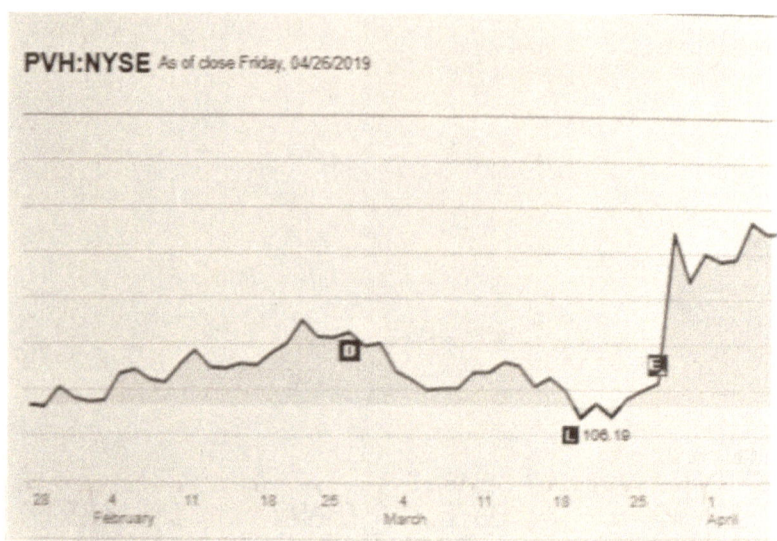

From Charles Schwab

E = EARNINGS ANNOUNCEMENT

SYMBOL	DATE	TRADE	DOLLARS
PVH	3/19	PURCHASE	$113.09
	3/21	SELL	$121.51
		PER SHARE PROFIT	$8.42

300 SHARE PROFIT x $58.32 = $17,496 - $10.00 = $17,486
Broker Fee & Exchange Commission = $10.00

EXHIBIT 8 - 31

PAYPAL (PYPL)

STOCK INVESTING GAME PLAN SELLING AFTER EARNINGS REPORT A
STOCK TRADING METHOD STOCK PRICE MOVEMENT

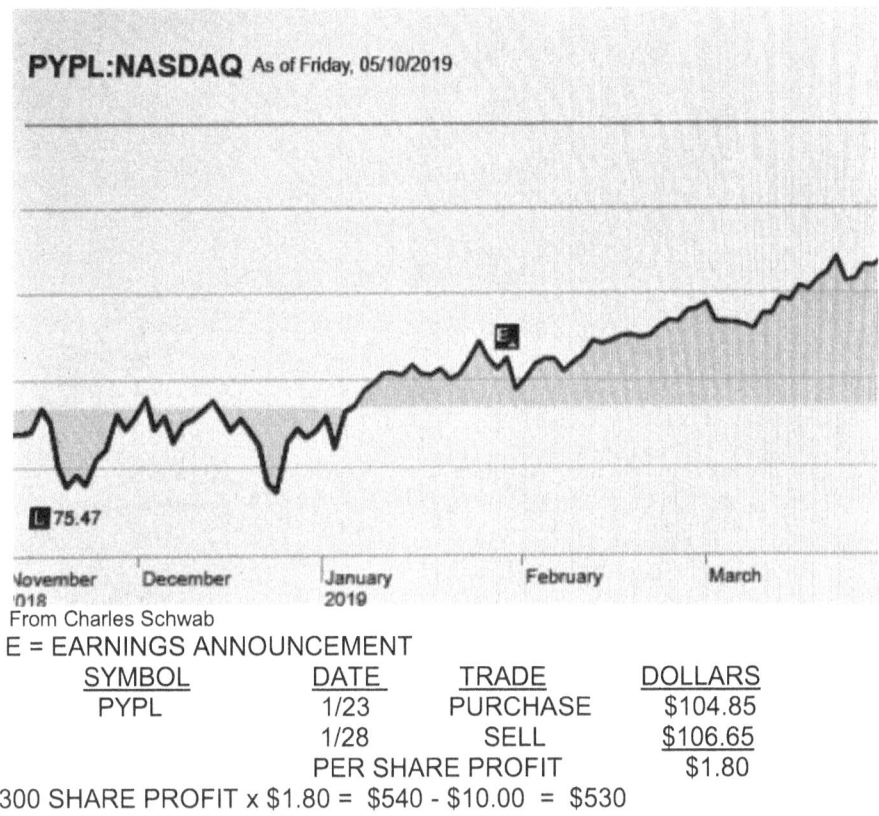

PYPL:NASDAQ As of Friday, 05/10/2019

L 75.47

November December January February March
2018 2019

From Charles Schwab

E = EARNINGS ANNOUNCEMENT

SYMBOL	DATE	TRADE	DOLLARS
PYPL	1/23	PURCHASE	$104.85
	1/28	SELL	$106.65
	PER SHARE PROFIT		$1.80

300 SHARE PROFIT x $1.80 = $540 - $10.00 = $530
Broker Fee & Exchange Commission = $10.00

EXHIBIT 8 - 32

ROST STORES (ROST)

STOCK INVESTING GAME PLAN SELLING AFTER EARNINGS REPORT A
STOCK TRADING METHOD STOCK PRICE MOVEMENT

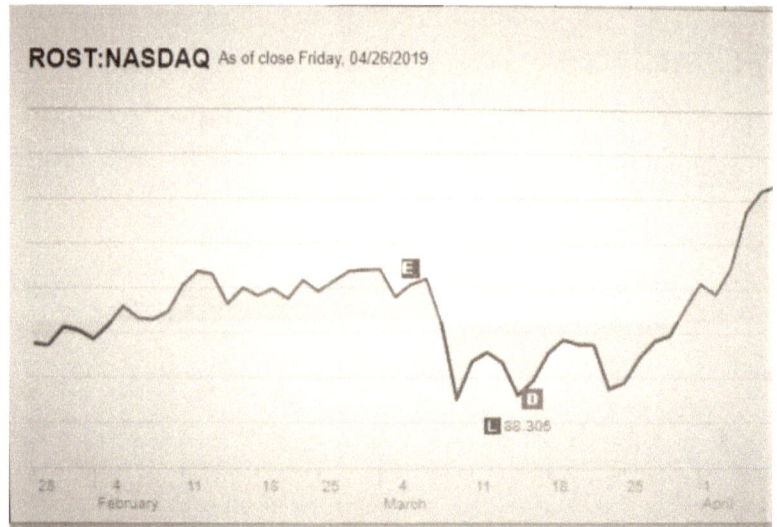

From Charles Schwab

E = EARNINGS ANNOUNCEMENT

SYMBOL	DATE	TRADE	DOLLARS
ROST	3/1	PURCHASE	$95.51
	3/6	SELL	$96.27
		PER SHARE PROFIT	$ .76

300 SHARE PROFIT x $.76 = $228 - $10.00 = $218.00
Broker Fee & Exchange Commission = $10.00

EXHIBIT 8 - 33

SMART (SMAR)

STOCK INVESTING GAME PLAN SELLING AFTER EARNINGS REPORT A
STOCK TRADING METHOD STOCK PRICE MOVEMENT

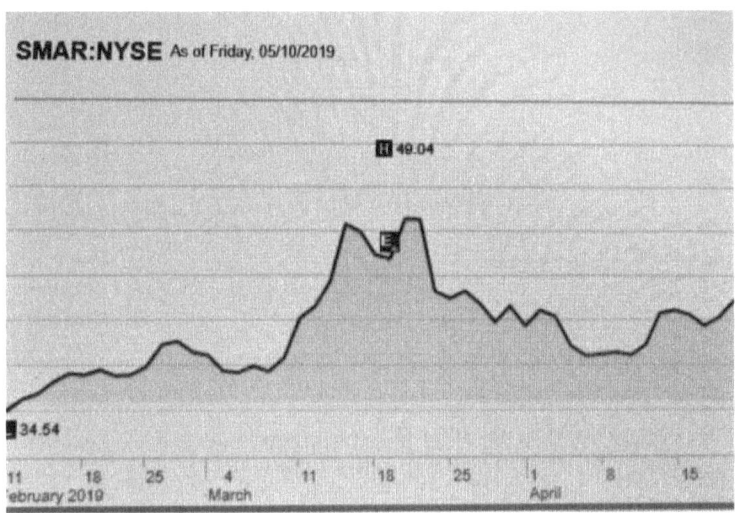

From Charles Schwab

E = EARNINGS ANNOUNCEMENT

SYMBOL	DATE	TRADE	DOLLARS
SMAR	3/18	PURCHASE	$45.45
	3/19	SELL	$46.75
	PER SHARE PROFIT		$1.29

300 SHARE PROFIT x $1.29 = $387 - $10.00 = $377
Broker Fee & Exchange Commission = $10.00

EXHIBIT 8 - 34

STITCH FIX (SFIX)

STOCK INVESTING GAME PLAN SELLING AFTER EARNINGS REPORT A
STOCK TRADING METHOD STOCK PRICE MOVEMENT

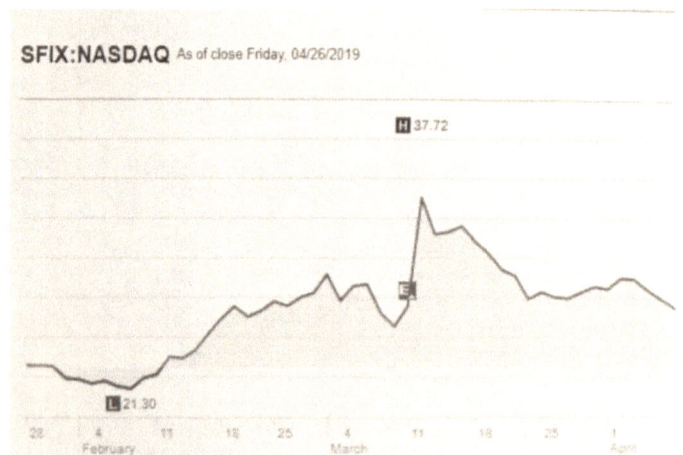

From Charles Schwab

E = EARNINGS ANNOUNCEMENT

SYMBOL	DATE	TRADE	DOLLARS
SFIX	3/6	PURCHASE	$28.43
	3/11	SELL	$35.51
		PER SHARE PROFIT	$7.08

300 SHARE PROFIT x $7.08 = $2,124 - $10.00 = $2,114.00
Broker Fee & Exchange Commission = $10.00

EXHIBIT 8 - 35

VISA (V)

STOCK INVESTING GAME PLAN SELLING AFTER EARNINGS REPORT A
STOCK TRADING METHOD STOCK PRICE MOVEMENT

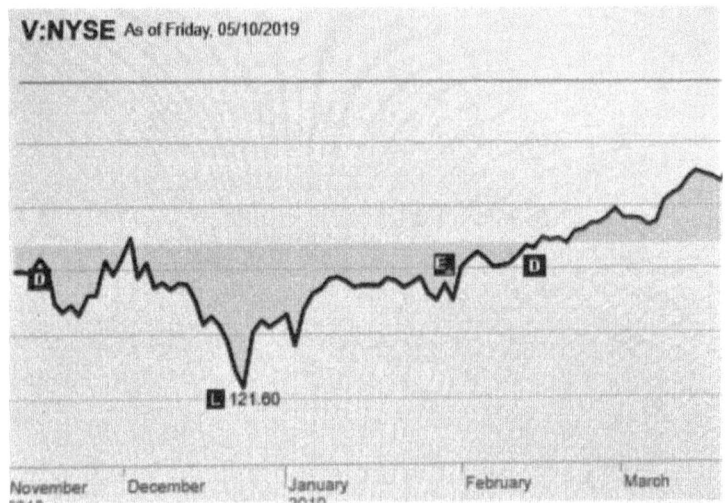

From Charles Schwab
E = EARNINGS ANNOUNCEMENT

SYMBOL	DATE	TRADE	DOLLARS
V	1/26	PURCHASE	$137.15
	2/1	SELL	$140.75
	PER SHARE PROFIT		$3.60

300 SHARE PROFIT 300 x $3.60 = $1,080 -$10.00 = $1.070
Broker Fee & Exchange Commission = $10.00

EXHIBIT 8 - 36

WEX INC. (WEX)

STOCK INVESTING GAME PLAN SELLING AFTER EARNINGS REPORT A
STOCK TRADING METHOD STOCK PRICE MOVEMENT

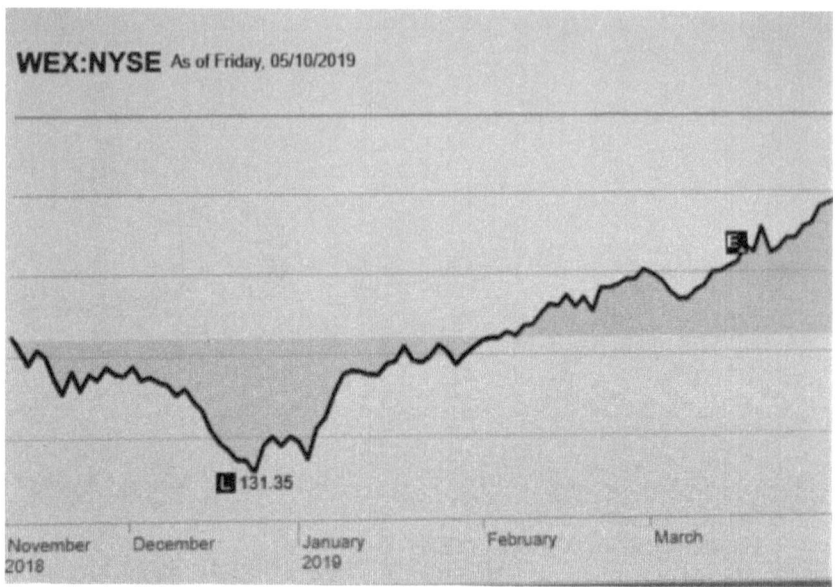

From Charles Schwab

E = EARNINGS ANNOUNCEMENT

SYMBOL	DATE	TRADE	DOLLARS
WEX	3/09	PURCHASE	$174.65
	3/13	SELL	$180.85
		PER SHARE PROFIT	$ 6.20

300 SHARE PROFIT x $6.20 = $1,860 - $10.00 = $1,850.00
Broker Fee & Exchange Commission = $10.00

106

CHAPTER 9

STOCK INVESTING GAME PLAN SELL AFTER EARNINGS REPORT A STOCK TRADING METHOD WORK SHEET

Stock Investing Game Plan Sell After Earnings Report A Stock Trading Method Work Sheet Trading Stocks
The third Stock Investing Game Plan Sell After Earnings Report a stock trading method tool is a stock Work Sheet. A stock Work Sheet is developed from your Final Note Pad. Each stock Work Sheet stock is best entered onto an Excel Computer Program but can be hand written. Each stock Work Sheet is uniquely title with a digital stock purchase trading day and earnings release day of a week. This feature is fundamental for your Completed Work Sheet record keeping.

To provide a complete understanding of a stock Work Sheet, the chapter presents 3 Work Sheets.

The first Work Sheet is a blank stock Work Sheet that provides a complete stock Work Sheet understanding and explanation for each stock entry (Exhibit 9 – 1).

The second Work Sheet is a partial complete stock Work Sheet. A partial complete Work Sheet has all your basic stock research information transferred from your stock Final Note Pad. This Final Note Pad stock transfer Work Sheet provides your stock information in a chronological sequence with an earnings release lowest digital numbered month with alpha character notation trading day release time before market (BM) as first, during market (DH) as second and after market (AF) as third and digital numbered of a month.

How To Complete Trading A Stock Investing Game Plan Sell After Earnings Report A Stock Trading Method Work Sheet
Each stock from your Final Note Pad is entered in the lowest to lowest digital earnings release month with alpha character notation trading day release time to highest digital earning release month your computer Sheet or written onto one line. The Work Sheet stock entry format has a stock (a) earnings release digital month notation, (b) earnings release digital day of a month with appropriate trading day earnings release time alpha character notation abbreviation (BM, DH or AF) and (c) two analyst earnings

estimates. From a calendar, you provide a stock earnings release alpha character day of a week notation and your anticipated stock share purchase quantity.

EXHIBIT 9 – 1

STOCK INVESTING GAME PLAN SELL AFTER EARNINGS REPORT
A STOCK TRADING METHOD BLANK WORK SHEET

Trading day to purchase stock
Earnings release day of month

(1)	(2)	(3)	(4)	(5)	(6)	(7)	(8)	(9)	(10)
DIGITAL									
MTH	ALPHA		ANALYST						
& DAY &	MTH		STK	STK		STK	STK	STK	STK
TRADE	DAY	STK	RANK	PRHSE	BKEN	MKT	GN/LS		GN/LS
TIME	DATE	SYM	(1)	(2)	#	$	$	$	%

COMMON STOCK DIGITAL PURCHASE DAY OF MONTH
COMMON STOCK DIGITAL EARNINGS RELEASE DAY OF MONTH
EARNINGS RELEASE TRADING DAY TIME ABBREVIATION (BM), (DH) & (AF)

(1) From common stock Final EPS Date Trading Method Note Pad

(2) From common stock Final EPS Date Trading Method Note Pad

(3) From common stock Final EPS Date Trading Method Note Pad

(4) From common stock Final EPS Date Trading Method Note Pad
(5) From common stock Final EPS Date Trading Method Note Pad
(6) You enter common stock purchase quantity
(7) Your enter common stock break-even dollar value

(8) After common stock sell, you enter your common stock
   market/sell dollar value

(9) Your computer calculates & enters

(10) Your computer calculates & enters

Your partial complete stock Work Sheet becomes complete after you transfer your broker stock purchase break-even price and sell trade transaction price. Your Stock Investing Game Plan Sell After Earnings Report A Stock trading method stock trading performance figures are transferred from your stock Computer Spread Sheet or entered into a partial complete Work Sheet computer that calculates for each stock your stock trading performance (See Exhibit 9 – 2).

The third stock Work Sheet is a stock Completed Work Sheet. To have a stock Completed Work Sheet requires you to complete for an earnings release day of a month all your stock purchase and sell trade transactions though your broker. After you complete your broker stock purchase and sell trade transactions notation options are two. These are (1) in your computer Work Sheet program you enter your broker stock (break-even) purchase and sell trade transaction prices or (2) from your stock Computer Spread Sheet you hand write or transfer to your stock Partial Completed Work Sheet. On your Partial Complete Work Sheet your broker stock purchase price is entered under a stock purchase (break-even) column and a stock sell trade transaction is entered under the market price column. Your computer completes all the necessary calculations to show your Stock Investing Game Plan Sell After Earnings Report A STOCK trading method stock trade performance. This calculation makes your Partial Completed Work Sheet a Completed Work Sheet.

The third stock Work Sheet is a stock Completed Work Sheet. To have a stock Completed Work Sheet requires you to complete for an earnings release day of a month all your stock purchase and sell trade transactions though your broker. After you complete your broker stock purchase and sell trade transactions notation options are two. These are (1) in your computer Work Sheet program you enter your broker stock (break-even) purchase and sell trade transaction prices or (2) from your stock Computer Spread Sheet you hand write or transfer to your stock Partial Completed Work Sheet.

On your Partial Complete Work Sheet your broker stock purchase price is entered under a stock purchase (break-even) column stock sell trade transaction is entered under the market price column. Your computer completes all the necessary calculations to show your Stock Investing Game Plan Sell After Earnings Report A stock trading method stock trade performance. This calculation makes your Partial Completed Work Sheet a Completed Work Sheet.

With each stock Work Sheet identified with earnings release day of month, it is a completed stock Work Sheet that is uniquely identified from other earnings release day stock Work Sheets. A complete stock Work Sheet becomes your record for a past day of a month earnings release trading performance and becomes a stock research source. (See Exhibit 9 – 3).

Stock Investing Game Plan Sell After Earnings Report A Stock Trading Method Review Of Each Stock Earnings Release Date

When using the Stock Investing Game Plan Sell After Earnings Report A Stock Trading Method, the author has experience after a Work Sheet completion that a stock can have a earnings release date change. This earnings release date change situation can occur in the short purchase window. It is suggested after you have completed your Work Sheet for each trading day of an earnings release month before a stock earnings release date you complete each stock earnings release date review and as required make (update) the appropriate changes to a stock earnings release date on your Work Sheet

EXHIBIT 9 – 2

STOCK INVESTING GAME PLAN SELL AFTER EARNINGS REPORT A STOCK TRADING METHOD PARTIAL COMPLETE WORK SHEET

1/5 DIGITAL PURCHASE DAY OF MONTH
1/9 DIGITAL EARNINGS RELEASE DAY OF MONTH

(1) DIGITAL ALPHA MTH & DAY TIME	(2) DAY DATE	(3) STK SYML	(4) ANYST RANK (1)	(5) (2)	(6) STK PRCHAS NBER #	(7) STK BRK/EVN $	(8) STK MKT $ $	(9) STK GN/LS $	(10) STK GN/LS %
1/9BM	MON	XYZ	3	**	300				
1/20DH	TUES	TOL	2	*	300				
1/30AF	WEDS	BA	1	**	300				
2/2DH	MON	AMZN	1	**	200				
2/2AF	MON	SPLK	1	**	300				
2/6AF	FRI	XLNX	2	**	300				
3/3BM	THUR	DER	3	*	300				
3/6DH	THUR	TEAM	2	**	300				

(7) Your enter common stock break-even dollar value
(8)   After common stock sell.you enter your common stock market/sell dollar value

(9) Your computer calculates & enters
(10) Your computer calculates & enters

EXHIBIT 9 – 3

STOCK INVESTING GAME PLAN SELL AFTER EARNINGS REPORT A STOCK TRADING METHOD COMPLETED WORK SHEET

1/5 DIGITAL PURCHASE DAY OF MONTH
1/9 DIGITAL EARNINGS RELEASE DAY OF MONTH

(1) DIGITAL MTH & DAY TRADE TIME	(2) ALPHA MTH DAY DATE	(3) STK SYML	(4) AYST STK RANK (1)	(5) PRHSE (2)	(6) STK #	(7) STK BKEVN $	(8) STK MKT $	(9) STK GN/LS $	(10) STK GN/LS %
1/9BM	MON	XYZ	3	**	300	75	67.1	7.90	.11
1/20DH	TUES	TOL	2	*	300	85	83.1	1.90	.02
1/30AF	WEDS	BA	1	**	300	345	310.1	34.90	.10
2/2DH	MON	AMZN	1	**	200	1377	1339.1	37.90	.03
2/2AF	MON	SPLK	1	**	300	133.	12.7	120.24	.90
2/6AF	FRI	XLNX	2	**	300	210	175.1	34.89	.17
3/3BM	THUR	DER	3	*	300	35	43.8	- 8.89	-.25
3/6DH	THUR	TEAM	2	**	300	97	91.4	5.57	.06

CHAPTER 10

WHEN TO SELL STOCK INVESTING GAME PLAN SELL AFTER EARNINGS REPORT TRADING METHOD STOCK

Sell Stock With Trading Stocks With Stock Investing Game Plan Sell After Earnings Report A Stock Trading Method
When to sell your Stock Investing Game Plan Sell After Earnings Report trading method stock share quantity is straight forward. It is based on a stock recent market price performance that is a reaction to corporate common stock earnings, earnings per share statement and corporate management guidance and a stock market price action that is compared to your stock market goal.
To sell through your stock broker your Stock Investing Game Plan Sell After Earnings Report trading method has several factors. These are (1) earnings release month and earnings release day of a month that are listed on your stock Work Sheet and stock Computer Spread Sheet, (2) earnings release trading day time such as Before Market Opens (BM), During Regular Trading Hours (RH) or After Market Closes (AF). These facts are listed on your stock Work Sheet and stock Computer Spread Sheet line and (3) your stock investment goals that has a stock market price increase above you stock purchase price that has a ($) flat dollar value price increase or percent return on invested dollars and sell your stock through your broker to make a profit.

When To Use One Or Both Investment Goals With Stock Investing Game Plan Sell After Earnings Report A Stock Trading Method There are two Stock Investing Game Plan Sell After Earnings Report trading method goals for your standards to maximize your stock market investing experience. There are many factors that motivate you to sell a stock and earn a profit.
   Your stock profit occurs after your broker sells your stock and a stock trade transaction price exceeds your stock broker stock break-even purchase trade transaction price. After these two prices are entered into your Computer Spread Sheet, it calculates your actual investment profit in terms or two investment goals as (1) flat dollar $ return and (2) percent % return on invested money. From these computer calculations and you selected profit

standard, you can determine that potential stock recent market sell transaction satisfies your profit standard.

But before you sell a stock, you have to anticipate your profits or returns. In your Computer Spread Sheet you have previously entered your broker stock (break-even) purchase price and next you enter your stock recent market price into your Computer Spread Sheet.

Your Computer Spread Sheet based on recent a stock market price, it calculates your anticipated profits in terms of two investment goals as (1) flat dollar $ return and (2) percent % return on invested money.

If you have a stock broker margin account, you have to pay a broker margin interest before you can claim a profit from Stock Investing Game Plan Sell After Earnings Report trading method investing. Per your broker margin agreement at the end of a month or you exceed your margin allowance, if you do not cover your interest dollar amount or margin allowance, then your required to add money to your stock account.

There are many factors that motivate you to sell a stock. These are (1) you need cash to cover your margin requirement or other expenses, then your sell a stock at the market price that is based on a flat dollar return, (2) you feel a stock price has completed a stock market price increase and it is below your % return goal, then your sell stock transaction is based on the flat dollar return, (3) apparent stock market risk factors, then your sell a stock that is based on the flat dollar return, (4) a stock recent market price has matched your profit expectations, then your sell a stock at the market price on a flat dollar or percent return, (5) a stock price has matched your analyst expectations, then your sell at the market price 50% of your stock quantity on a flat dollar retain the other 50% of your stock quantity for a percent return and (6) with a low price stock, large stock market price increases do not occur many occasions, then sell at a flat dollar profit or as it meets your profit % return and with high stock market price stock, large price increases occur more frequent the sell at a flat dollar profit or % return.

Other factors that determine when to sell your Stock Investing Game Plan Sell After Earnings Report trading method stocks are several. These factors are (1) day number to sell an earnings release stock is 4 to 5 days or more days after your broker stock

purchase. Your broker stock purchase an earnings release stock occurs 3 to 4 days or more days prior to a stock earnings release date. When a stock earnings release occurs on a stock next trading (earnings release) day, if your stock market price increase is above your purchase price and matches your investment goal, you sell your stock through a broker.
(See Exhibit 10 – 1)

EXHIBIT 10 – 1

STOCKS INVESTING GAME PLAN SELL AFTER EARNINGS A STOCK TRADING METHOD STOCK PURCHASE & SELL TIME PERIOD

PURCHASE STOCK HOLD DAYS	SELL STOCK SELL DAYS
3 TO 4 DAYS OR MORE DAYS BEFORE EARNINGS RELEASE DAY OF MONTH YOU HOLD YOUR STOCK	AFTER EARNINGS RELEASE SELL YOUR STOCK EQUALS 1 TO 2 DAYS AFTER EARNINGS RELEASE DAY OF MONTH

Earnings release is a corporation's report that shows its past quarter earnings/sales as a beat or miss. If a corporation earnings release and earnings per share are a beat then it is preferred for you due a stock market price increase is above your purchase price and it matches your investment goal and you sell your stock through your stock broker and add to your profits. If a corporation earnings release statement and earnings per share beats an analyst group forecast, then a stock market price should increase above your purchase price and match you investment goal and you sell your stock through your stock broker at a profit. If a corporation earnings release and earnings per share are a miss then it is not preferred for your stock due a stock market price decrease that is below your purchase price, you sell your stock through your stock broker or you wait for the next trading session and hope you realize a slight stock market price increase and sell your stock through you broker with a lower loss against your profits. If a corporation earnings release statement and earnings per share misses the analyst group forecast, then a stock market price should decrease is below your purchase price and does not

match your investment goal, you sell your stock through your stock broker at a loss or (2) you wait for the next trading section and hope you realize a slight stock market price increase and sell your stock through you broker with a lower loss
against your profits.

Trading Stocks With Stock Investing Game Plan Sell After Earnings Report A Stock Trading Method Stock Sell Factors
The second Stock Investing Game Plan Sell After Earnings Report trading method component group is your stock sell criteria. Your sell stock criteria are the bases for your stock share quantity sell trade transactions and are straight forward. Your stock sell criteria is based on your stock investment goal and broker stock market purchase and stock market sell prices that determines your profit or loss. Your investment goals are what motivate you to invest (purchase) with a Stock Investing Game Plan Sell After Earnings Report trading method
in the stock market and triggers you to have your broker stock sell transaction.

During a stock trading day to obtain a most recent stock market price, you access your stock broker program or cell phone app stock market section or obtain a stock market price from a TV business program such as CNBC stock symbol ticker price or news alert. (See Exhibit 10 – 2)

The first stock sell transaction factor is a stock earnings beat, earnings per share beat and strong corporate management guidance or other event that increases a stock market price above your purchase (break-even) stock market price, then you sell at the market price your stock through your stock broker your stock at a profit. To protect a stock profit you sell a stock at stock market price or if you have some flexibility to sell your stock through your stock broker at a stock limit (ask) market price that is slightly higher than a stock current market price then you complete a broker stock sell transaction. In the stock market, there are several stock earnings release situations that impact your stock market price. One situation is a common stock earnings release had good earnings and excellent earnings per share, but management gave poor or weak future corporate business guidance. This situation has a stock market price decrease below your purchase price that does not match your investment goal, then you sell at the market price your stock through your stock broker within the present trading day at the present stock market price or wait for the next stock trading session that could have a slight stock market price increase and you sell your stock through your broker.

The second stock situation is that a stock earnings increase, earnings per share beat or strong corporate guidance or other event to increases a stock market price. The stock market price increase is above your purchase price and matches your investment goal (1) flat dollar $ profit per stock or (2) price increase as a percent % return on your stock investment. When your stock market price increase exceeds or matches your stock investment goal, then you sell stock at the market price your stock through your broker account at the stock market price and take a profit. To protect a stock profit you sell through your broker a stock at market price or if you have some flexibility to sell at a stock limit (ask) price that could be slightly higher than a stock current market price.

Exhibit 10 – 2

CNBC TV PROGRAM TICKER TAPE

From CNBC TV

It is noted that to protect your investment money sum, with a stock price loss, you sell your stock through your broker account at the market price or you wait for the next stock trading session that could have a slightly stock market price.

Your flat dollar ($) price gain and % percent return on your invested money ($) options your options are (1) if you feel that a stock has a low probability for additional $ dollar gains or based on your investor's gut feel, then you sell at the market price your stock through your stock broker, (2) if you feel that a stock has a good potential to have additional stock market price increase (additional $ dollar gains), then your stock sell options are (a) do not sell your stock at the present stock market price but retain your stock share quantity for additional $ dollar gains and then at the new stock market price sell your stock through your broker or (b) sell one half (50 percent) of your stock quantity at the present stock market price to get the profits but retain the other half of your stock share quantity for additional $ dollar gains. As your stock market price increases you sell at the new stock market price your stock through your stock broker at a higher stock market price.

If you deviate from your investment goals, objectives or practices such as going for the pot of gold, then you increase your potential to have a stock trading loss. Remember an old saying Pigs get fat and Hogs get slathered or it is better to have a piece of pie than no pie.

The third stock situation is that a stock had an earnings release decrease, missed earnings per share, poor corporate management guidance. This situation decreases a stock market price below your purchase price and below your investment goal and you have a stock expected dollar loss. To protect your money (funds) from a stock lose then (1) you sell your stock through your stock broker at stock current market price at a loss or (2) you wait for the next stock trading session that could have a slightly stock market price.

When To Sell Your Stock At A Loss With Stock Investing Game Plan Sell After Earnings Report A Stock Trading Method
After you enter a stock recent market price in your Computer Spread Sheet and it that calculates to a potential lose, you have basically two stock sell decisions. These are (1) to hold a stock and hope that in the future a stock will have a stock market price increase that allows you to sell a stock through your broker for a

profit or (2) to sell a stock at the present market price and take a stock loss and on your taxes to take a stock sold lose against your stock sold profits.

With the Federal Tax Policy, if you sell a stock (s) for a profit (2) and some stock (s) is sold at a loss, then the stock lose (s) are applied against your stock sold profits: thereby reducing your taxable income. If your sold stock profit (s) are in excess of your stock sold loss (s), you can apply $3,000 of the excess sold stock loss (s) to other income to reduce your annual taxes.

A fourth stock situation is a stock market price that allows your retail stock trade transaction through your broker to be completed on time. Stock sell dollar end digit transaction dollar amounts are (1) your stock sell transaction price ends has a last digit number as an odd digit 1, 3, 5, 7 or 9. If your stock transaction has an odd digit last number (Example is $409.00 or $409.01), your stock sell trade transaction has a greater potential to be completed due to the fact that most retail stock investors use a stock transaction dollar number that ends with an even digit. This feature means that your broker stock sell trade transaction price has you ahead of the herd or (2) your stock sell transaction ends with a dollar last digit number as an even digit 2, 4, 6, 8, 0 Example is $48.00 or $49.02). If there are a great number of retail stock investors with market sell transactions that end with even digits, then your stock sell trade transaction could be delayed or completed a lower dollar per stock share.

CHAPTER 11

STOCK INVESTING GAME PLAN SELL AFTER EARNINGS REPORT A STOCK TRADING METHOD COMPUTER SPREAD SHEET

Stock Investing Game Plan Sell After Earnings Report A Stock Trading Method Computer Spread Sheet
The fourth Stock Investing Game Plan Sell After Earnings Report a stock trading method tool is your stock Computer Spread Sheet. Your Computer Spread Sheet is considered your tool (form) for your stock trading road map or stock trading platform does two important functions. These are (1) with a recent stock market price to estimate your potential stock profit and (2) after a stock sell transaction by your broker, it tracks your Stock Investing Game Plan Sell After Earnings Report a stock trading method stock trading performance. For your daily trading activity, a stock Computer Spread Sheet is computer based or paper printed. It is most important Stock Investing Game Plan Sell After Earnings Report a stock trading method tool due to allows you with a recent stock market price to show your potential profit.

On your stock Computer Spread Sheet, there is one column for each stock earnings release digital month notation with some additional space (9/21--) and earnings release digital day of a month date notation. It is noted that a stock earnings release digital day of a month column notation has additional width to list a stock earnings release trading day time. The trading day earning release time is an alpha character notation of (BM, DH or AF) and is adjacent to the digital day of a month notation.

Another stock Computer Spread Sheet column has from a calendar you enter a stock earnings release alpha character notation for day of a week such as (MON, TUES, WEDS, THURS or FRI). The earnings release day of a week alpha character notation is separate and helps make you (trader) aware of a stock earnings release trading day. A stock earnings release day of a month is a calendar date that you must own a stock and you can sell your stock through your broker and make a profit. The next column is for a stock symbol that you obtain from your Work Sheet.

Two other columns are (1) from your stock Work Sheet, there is one column for two analyst earnings estimates and (2) a second column for you to enter your anticipated stock share purchase quantity. (See Exhibit 11 – 1)

EXHIBIT 11 – 1

STOCK INVESTING GAME PLAN SELL AFTER EARNINGS REPORT
A STOCK TRADING METHOD BLANK
COMPUTER SPREAD SHEET

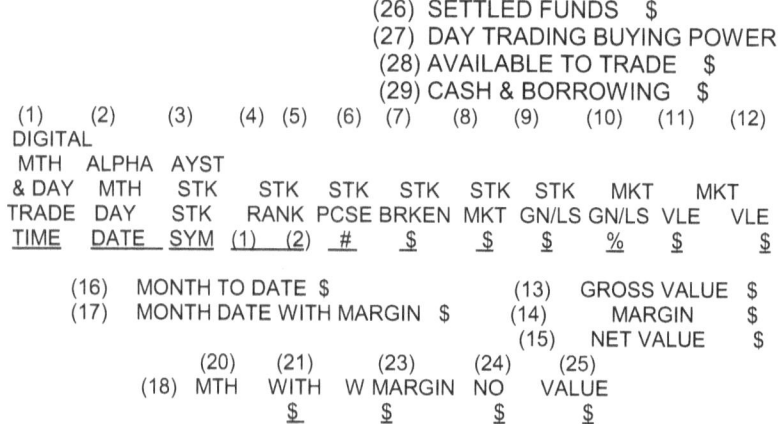

SPREAD SHEET IDENTIFICATION LEGEND

A spread sheet identification legend explains each entry you will make to a computer spread sheet and the figures that are calculated by your computer.

1. Stock anticipated earnings release from Work Sheet digital number with earnings release digital month, earnings release digital day of month & alpha character abbreviation for earnings release time of day
2. Alpha character for earnings release day of week, from Work Sheet
3. Stock Symbol you enter from Work Sheet
4. Analysts one stock and earnings release ranking from Work Sheet
5. Analysts two stock and earnings release ranking from Work Sheet
6. Stock purchase quantity from Work Sheet
7. Stock break-even purchase price you calculate from your

broker trade purchase price

8. Stock sell (market) price. In a trading day, there are two entries in the column. The first entry is a stock market price to determine your potential profit.
9. Second entry is to enter your broker trade sell transaction that show your actual profit
10. Flat dollar ($) per stock gain or loss, computer calculates from stock broker break-even purchase price and stock market recent price or your broker stock sell price
10. Stock percent (%) per stock gain or loss, computer calculates
11. Stock value computer calculates a stock share quantity multiplied by most a stock recent market price or broker sell transaction stock price to show stock shares value,
12. Portfolio market value is a stock share quantity multiplied times most recent stock market price to show contribution to your stock broker portfolio, computer calculates
13. Gross value computer calculates your total stock portfolio value,
14. Margin dollar amount from your broker account you enter
15. Net value dollar amount is your portfolio account value less margin value computer calculates
16. Month to date total stock value shows your stock investment value month to date, computer calculates
17. Month to date total stock value shows your stock investment value month to date, after margin amount entry computer calculates
18. Each month is the month of year, you enter
19. Each month margin amount is from broker account, you enter
20. Each month stock value total, you enter from (16)
21. Each month stock value total less margin amount from your broker, you enter from (17)
22. Year to date stock value total less margin is present month from (17) added to previous month stock value (20)
23. Year to date stock value total is present month from (16) added to previous month stock value (19)
24. Settled funds are from your broker account and shows

available funds for you to complete checks
25. Day trading buying power funds available to a day trader
26. Available to trade are funds available to a day trader
27. Cash and borrowing are funds available to a person with a broker margin account to purchase stock.

How To Complete Your Stock Investing Game Plan Sell After Earnings Report A Stock Trading Method Computer Spread Sheet After your transfer each stock earnings release day of a month, symbol, earnings estimates and stock purchase quantity from your Work Sheet directly to your stock Computer Spread Sheet computer, you have a Partial Completed Computer Spread Sheet. (See Exhibit 11 – 2)

After you complete a broker stock purchase, you enter your broker stock purchase market price as your stock break-even price that combines your broker stock transaction price, broker commissions and project exchange fee. With your stock break-even purchase price and recent stock market price entered in your computer, your computer projects your stock price potential profit or loss. If your stock potential gain exceeds or matches your investment goal, then you sell your stock through your broker. After a broker stock sell transaction price entry into your computer, your computer calculates based on your broker sell stock market price your Stock Investing Game Plan Sell After Earnings Report a stock trading method trading profits.

On a stock Computer Spread Sheet, your computer calculates your stock flat dollar ($) profit and percent % return on investment. With your stock recent market price, a Computer Spread Sheet is considered your stock investment road map that shows based on a stock recent market price that is above your stock purchase price and is your
potential profit or loss. After you complete your stock sell transaction through your broker, you enter a stock actual sell trade transaction price in a market column to show an actual stock sell transaction price.

Earnings Release Day Qualified Stock Number For A Trading Day Of A Month Listed On Stock Investing Game Plan Sell After Earnings Report A Stock Trading Method Computer Spread Sheet Factors

Your number of earnings release day qualified stocks for a trading day of a month is listed on your computer spread sheet varies per trading day. The number of qualified stocks varies per day or week due to number of Stock Investing Game Plan Sell After Earnings Report trading method qualified stocks per week and per day. It is noted that during earnings season (high number of stocks reporting earnings) there is a potential high number of stock having earnings releases per day.

It has been the author's experience to have at have 3 to 4 and as high as 10 stock earning release days per page. This feature provides you with your stock trading picture for a day and maybe a week. With a day or week trading picture and computer spread sheet shows each stock (1) earnings release digital day of a month and day of a week with its alpha earnings release time of a trading day and (2) day of week alpha character shows that trading day that has a trader aware of a day and week stock trading activity.

EXHIBIT 11 – 2

STOCK INVESTING GAME PLAN SELL AFTER EARNINGS REPORT A STOCK TRADING METHOD PARTIAL COMPLETE COMPUTER SPREAD SHEET

1/5 DIGITAL PURCHASE DAY OF MONTH
1/9 DIGITAL EARNINGS RELEASE DAY OF MONTH

(1) DIGITAL MTH & DAY & TRADE TIME	(2) ANALYST MTH DAY DATE	(3) STK STK SYM	(4) STK RANK (1)	(5) (2)	(6) STK PCHSE #	(7) STK BREVEN $	(8) STK MARKET $	(9) STK GN/LS $	(10) STK GN/LS %
1/9BM	MON	XYZ	3	**	300				
1/20DH	TUES	TOL	2	*	300				
1/30AF	WEDS	BA	1	**	300				
2/2DH	MON	AMZN	1	**	200				
2/2AF	MON	SPLK	1	**	300				
2/6AF	FRI	XLNX	2	**	300				
3/3BM	THUR	DER	3	*	300				
3/6DH	THUR	TEAM	2	**	300				

(7) Your enter common stock break-even dollar value
(8) After common stock sell. you enter your common stock market/sell dollar value
(9) Your computer calculates & enters
(10) Your computer calculates & enters

With several weeks of stock earnings release days within a week on a computer spread sheet after you enter a broker stock sell transaction onto a computer spread sheet and work sheet, you delete a sold stock from your Computer Spread Sheet. A sold stock deletion reduces the number of stock earnings release days on a computer spread sheet and allows a trader to focus on the next day of a week earning release stocks.

From your Work Sheet do not delete any broker stock trade transaction purchase or sell prices due to it is each stock earnings release day trading performance record.

To facilitate navigating through an earnings release month, earnings release day of a month and earnings release time of trading day your stocks are listed on your stock Computer Spread Sheet. As you enter a stock recent market sell price, to show a stock profit or loss above a stock purchase price it is recommended to have different stock Computer Spread Sheet sections as color coded to show a profit or loss. Color coded sections provide you with a quick reference. It is been the author's practice to have a stock Computer Spread Sheet with one bright color. The bright color shows a profit from a stock market recent price or broker actual stock sell price. When you use a yellow color to show a profit from a stock market sell price or broker actual stock sell price, then all stocks with stock recent market price increases above your purchase prices and meet or exceed your investment goal have a yellow highlight and are quickly identified.

A second less bright color shows a loss from a stock recent market potential price or broker actual stock sell price. If you use a light brown or purple color to show a loss from a stock recent market sell price or broker actual stock sell price, you can quickly identify stocks that do meet you investment goal.

Another colored code feature is to have your present trading day digital and alpha character earnings release dates in a light color. This feature helps a trader (you) become aware of stocks that have earnings release during a trading day.

To become aware of a stock earnings release, you listen to or watch CNBC TV, Bloomberg TV, cell phone or Yahoo finance. Included in a stock earnings release statement is a stock earnings,

earnings per share release and corporate management guidance. From these stock research sources you obtain a recent stock market price that you enter into your stock Computer Spread Sheet under a stock market price column.   After a stock market price entry, your computer program calculates your potential stock flat dollar $ increase or % return on invested $ dollars. If a recent stock market sell price increase is above your purchase price and it matches your investment goal, then you sell your stock through your stock broker and pocket the profits. If there is a stock recent market price decrease that is below your purchase price, then you sell your stock through your stock broker at the market price and incur a loss or wait for another trading session. (See Exhibit 11 – 3).

  After your broker completes a stock sell transaction, you verify a broker sell stock price is the same as your sell price that was entered into your computer. If there is different broker stock market sell price, then you enter a broker stock sell transaction stock into your computer.

EXHIBIT 11 – 3

STOCK INVESTING GAME PLAN SELL AFTER EARNINGS REPORT
A STOCK TRADING METHOD COMPLETE COMPUTER SPREAD
SHEET

SETTLED FUNDS
DAY TRADING BUYING POWER
AVAILABLE TO TRADE
CASH & BORROWING

(1) DIGITAL MTH DAY & MTH TRADE TIME	(2) ALPHA DAY DATE	(3) STK STK SYML (1)	(4) STK RANK (2)	(5) STK PCHSE #	(6) STK BK N $	(7) STK MKT $	STK GN/LS $	(8) STK GN/LS %	(9) MKT VLE $	(10) VLE $
		ANALYST								
1/9BM	MON	XYZ	3 **	300	75	67.1	7.90	.11	2370	22500
1/20DH	TUES	TOL	2 *	300	85	83.1	1.90	.02	570	25500
1/30AF	WEDS	BA	1 **	300	345	310.1	34.90	.10	10470	103500
2/2DH	MON	AMZN	1 **	200	1377	1339.1	37.90	.03	7580	275400
2/2AF	MON	SPLK	1 **	300	133	12.7	120.24	.90	36072	39900
2/6AF	FRI	XLNX	2 **	300	210	175.1	34.89	.17	10467	63000
3/3BM	THUR	DER	3 *	300	35	43.8	- 8.89	-.25	-2667	10500
3/6DH	THUR	TEAM	2 **	300	97	91.4	5.57	.06	1671	29100

MONTH TO DATE 66533   GROSS VALUE 66533   569400
MONTH DATE WITH MARGIN   61643   MARGIN   -4890
                         NET VALUE   564510

	MONTH MARGIN $	WITH MARGIN $	W MARGIN YTD $	NO MARGIN $	YTD $
MONTH					

Your stock Computer Spread Sheet is updated with all earnings release day broker stocks purchase and sell prices. Your computer calculates your stocks flat dollar ($) and (%) percent return on investment statistics and other trading performance indicators.

Next, on your stock Computer Spread Sheet you complete all your necessary dollar profit or loss entries to the year to date (YTD) profit/loss sections, month to date (MTD) profit sections and funds available to withdraw or trade. With a margin account you update all the year to date final trading figures and to the settled cash and funds available to trade figures.

A stock Computer Spread Sheet year to date statistics are (1) stock portfolio value and margin value, (2) Stock Investing Game Plan Sell After Earnings Report a stock trading method stock trading value and (3) Stock Investing Game Plan Sell After Earnings Report trading method stock value less margin value.

After you enter your broker stock sell transaction price into your partial completed Work Sheet, you verify all earnings release day stock purchase price and sell price entries. This assures you have an accurate record for each stock earnings release trading performance and your computer spread sheet can be updated. Your stock Work Sheet becomes your earnings release trading day of a month record and becomes a stock research source. Since your stock Computer Spread Sheet is a fluid instrument that handles one or two earnings release days of a month stocks, sold stocks are removed from a stock Computer Spread Sheet. This creates space for your stock Computer Spread Sheet next earnings release day of a month or new stocks.

CHAPTER 12

STOCK INVESTING GAME PLAN SELL AFTER EARNINGS A STOCK TRADING METHOD COMPLETED WORK SHEETS RECORD KEEPING

Stock Investing Game Plan Sell After Earnings Report A Stock Trading Method Completed Work Sheet Is Your Stock Trading Record

Your completed Stock Investing Game Plan Sell After Earnings Report a stock trading method Work Sheet becomes a (your) stock past or completed Stock Investing Game Plan Sell After Earnings Report a stock trading method stock research source. This is the reason each Work Sheet is uniquely titled with an earnings release day of month and purchase day of a month. A completed Work Sheet shows how each stock performed for a past earnings release day of a month. Your Work Sheet shows each stock (1) broker break-even purchase trade $ price, (2) broker sell (market) trade $ price, (3) flat dollar $ as profit and (4) percent % as a return to invested dollars. These stock facts are very important as your future stock research facts. These facts show each stock performance on a previous earnings release day and allows you to rank each stock based on earnings release of a day stocks past performance (best to lowest) such as flat ($) dollar and & percent on invested dollars.

   This feature allows you to develop your top 200 hundred stocks for a year that could repeat every 3 months.

   Since all corporations are required to issue earnings releases every 3 months, your stock completed Work Sheet shows how well each common stock performed. With some stock earnings release slight variances due to calendar days and corporation selected earnings release date, a stock earnings release is scheduled for 3 months later. This provides you with a stock list that you can focus your additional stock research. An every 3 groups of 4 month earnings release schedule has are group into month groups. These four month groups are Group 1 months for potential stock repeat earnings release January, April, July & October, Group 2 months for potential stock repeat earnings

release are February, May, August & November and Group 3 months
are for potential stock repeat earnings release March, June, September & December. (See Exhibit 12 – 1)

EXHIBIT 12 – 1

STOCK INVESTING GAME PLAN SELL AFTER EARNINGS REPORT
A STOCK TRADING METHOD ANTICIPATING A STOCK TO REPEAT
EARNINGS BY MONTH GROUPING

GROUP 1	GROUP 2	GROUP 3
JANUARY (1)	FEBRUARY (2)	MARCH (3)
APRIL (4)	MAY (5)	JUNE (6)
JULY (7)	AUGUST (8)	SEPTEMBER (9)
OCTOBER (10)	NOVEMBER (11)	DECEMBER (12)

CHAPTER 13

STOCK INVESTING GAME PLAN SELL AFTER EARNINGS REPORT A STOCK TRADING METHOD RESEARCH SOURCES

Stock Investing Game Plan Sell After Earnings Report A Stock Trading Method Research Sources

Stock Investing Game Plan Sell After Earnings Report a stock trading method research sources are an important basic component to have a successful and profitable Stock Investing Game Plan Sell After Earnings Report a stock trading method strategy or future experience. Your stock research sets your Stock Investing Game Plan Sell After Earnings Report a stock trading method in motion with your broker purchase stock price entered in your computer. On a stock earnings release trading day recent market stock price entry in your computer determines your potential profit or loss and your broker selling your stock. With a broker actual stock sell price entered into your computer, it shows your actual profit or loss. This is an excellent stock research for the next earnings month.

From your basic stock research (free on the internet) you obtain stock symbols. Your stock research has each symbol related earnings release trading month, earnings release day of a month, earnings release trading day of a week, and earnings release trading day time and analyst earnings projection or estimate. With this stock research information, you determine your qualified stocks for your Stock Investing Game Plan Sell After Earnings Report a stock trading method stock earnings release trading day activity.

Your stock research sources includes (1) corporate earnings report, (2) calendar of corporate earnings, (3) articles that review a corporation or corporate earnings, earnings per share and management corporate guidance. If there occurs a corporate news release that cause a stock market price movement, then based on your investment goal, you sell your stock shares through your broker, (4) articles from financial companies, stock broker firms, newspapers, magazines, TV programs and internet and your past completed Stock Investing Game Plan Sell After Earnings Report a stock trading method Work Sheets.

A very important stock information fact is a stock recent stock market price. Your stock market price information sources are from your stock broker program, cell phone or ticker tape, a ticker tape on TV program that appears screen along a TV screen bottom. The ticker tape has stock market price news streaming on time and shows a stock market price. A stock market price options are (1) stock symbol in red with a stock recent market price dollar decline, (2) stock symbol white for no stock recent market price movement, (3) stock symbol green for a stock recent market price dollar increase and (4) CNBC streaming ticker tape. If there is a tremendous stock market price movement, a TV commenter reviews a stock market price movement.
(See Exhibit 13 – 1)

EXHIBIT 13 -1

CNBC TV Program Stock Price Ticker

From CNBC TV

Some of the various stock research sources are (1) paper printed resource that includes newspapers, magazines, newsletters (2) free on the internet includes Zacks, GOOGL, Yahoo, & Bloomberg research that includes articles, stock broker program research, (3) TV research includes programs with commenter and ticker tapes and (4) ticker tape. (See Exhibit 13 – 2 and Exhibit 13 – 3)

EXHIBIT 13 – 2

STOCK INVESTING GAME PLAN SELL AFTER EARNINGS REPORT
A STOCK TRADING METHOD STOCK RESEARCH RESOURCES
  BENZINGA
  BLOOMBERG
  FORBES
  GOOGL
  INVESTING
  INVESTOPEDIA
  INVESTORS BUSINESS DAILY
  KIPLINGER
  MARKET CHANELEON
  MARKET INSIDER
  MORINGSTAR
  MOTLEY FOOL
  NASDAQ
  REUTERS
  YAHOO
  ZACKS INVESTMENT RESEARCH

EXHIBIT 13 – 3

STOCK INVESTING GAME PLAN SELL AFTER EARINGS REPORT A
STOCK TRADING METHOD STOCK EARNINGS RELEASES &
CALENDAR OF EARNINGS RESEARCH SOURCES
  BLOOMBERG
  GOOGL
  INFOSPACE
  INSIDER
  INVESTORS BUSINESS DAILY
  KENSAQ
  KIPLINGER
  MARKETCHAMELEON
  MARKETSBUSINESS
  MORNINGSTAR
  SCHWAB
  SEEKING ALPHA
  YAHOO
  YOUR BROKER
  ZACKS INVESTMENT RESEARCH

ZACKs EARNINGS REPORT PAGE
After on the chrome or internet browser, you enter Zacks to
access the various Zacks stock research reports and Zacks
earnings report page. The Zack's earnings report is a one page

report. Next, you enter a stock symbol into the upper right box to obtain a stock earnings page that has one page. We use three pages to show the information. The information is (1) company name, (2) recent stock market price and price change, (3) earnings release numerical ranking of 1, 2, 3, 4, or 5, digital notation for earnings release month and day of month, (4) if available earnings release trading
day time. If a stock earnings release occurs in regular trading hours there is - or no alpha character notation before a stock digital day of month. If a stock has BEFORE(BM) trading hours earnings release then there is a BEFORE alpha character notation before a stock digital day of month. If a stock has AFTER trading hours earnings release there is an AFTER (AF) alpha character notation before a stock digital day of month, (5) stock industry ranking position as % to the total, (6) stocks industry sector ranking % of the total and (7) other important stock financial information.

EXHIBIT 13 – 4

ZACKS EARNINGS REPORT

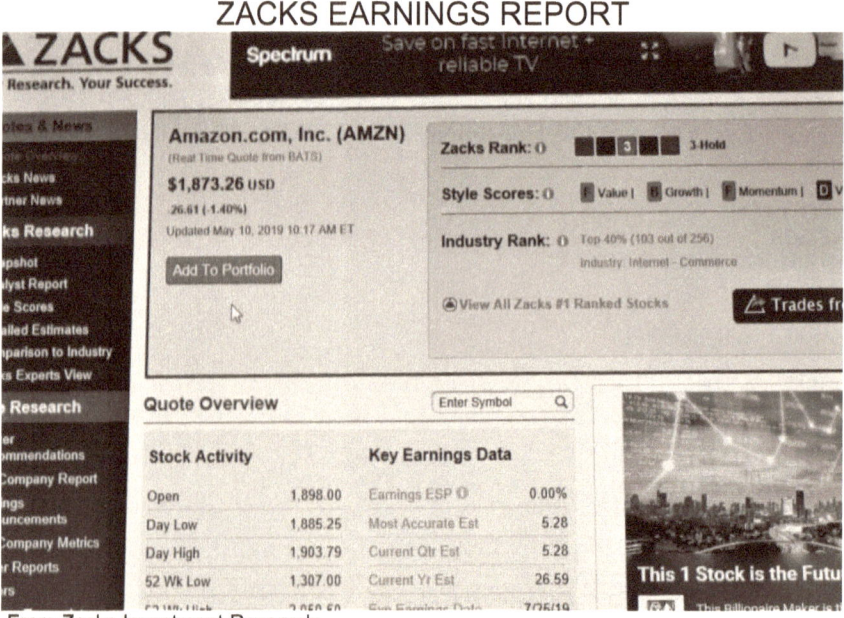

From Zacks Investment Research

ZACKS EARNINGS REPORT Continued

Stock Activity			Key Earnings Data	
Open	1,898.00		Earnings ESP ⓞ	0.00%
Day Low	1,885.25		Most Accurate Est	5.28
Day High	1,903.79		Current Qtr Est	5.28
52 Wk Low	1,307.00		Current Yr Est	26.59
52 Wk High	2,050.50		Exp Earnings Date	7/25/19
Avg. Volume	4,172,141		Prior Year EPS	20.14
Market Cap	935.37 B		Exp EPS Growth (3-5yr)	33.05%
Dividend	0.00 (0.00%)		Forward PE	71.44
Beta	1.62		PEG Ratio	2.16

Retail-Wholesale » Internet - Commerce

This 1 Stock is th

This Billionaire
one stock of th

Price and EPS Sur

1 Month | 3 Months | YTD

EPS Surprise ♦ ♦

Research Reports for AMZN

Analyst 🔲   Snapshot 🔲   ⓐ All Zacks' Analyst Reports »

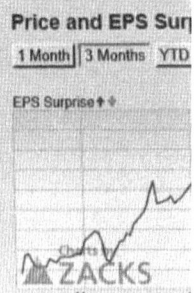

News for AMZN

ZACKS EARNINGS REPORT Continued

Premium Research for AMZN

Zacks Rank ⓞ	▼ Hold 3
Zacks Industry Rank ⓞ	Top 40% (103 out of 256)
Zacks Sector Rank ⓞ	Bottom 44% (9 out of 16)
Style Scores ⓞ	F Value | B Growth | F Momentum | D VGM
Earnings ESP ⓞ	0.00%
Research Reports for AMZN ⓞ	Analyst | Snapshot

(▲ ▼ = Change in last 30 days)

ⓐ View All Zacks Rank #1 Strong Buys

ZACKS EARNINGS PAGE

Zacks earnings page shows (1) top stocks expected to have a trading day earnings beat, (2) earnings analysis and (3) stock earnings ESP (expected surprise earnings stocks).

EXHIBIT 13 – 5
ZACKS EARNINGS PAGE

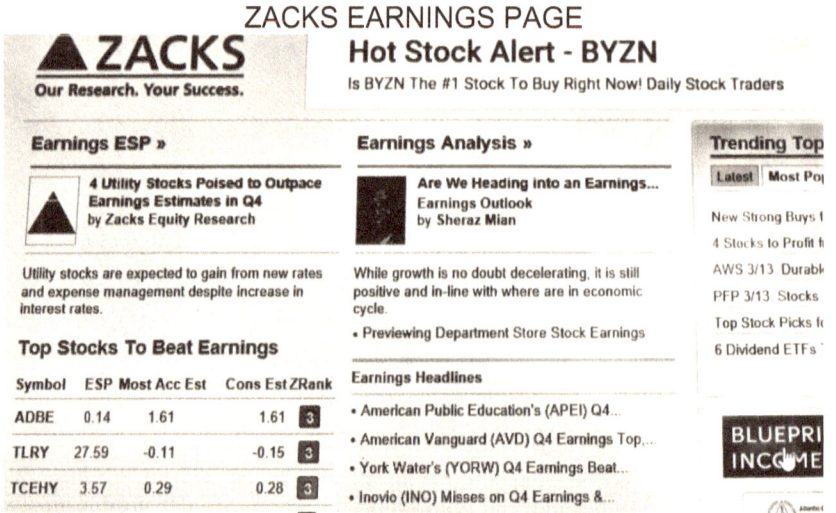

ZACKS
Our Research. Your Success.

Hot Stock Alert - BYZN
Is BYZN The #1 Stock To Buy Right Now! Daily Stock Traders

Earnings ESP »

4 Utility Stocks Poised to Outpace Earnings Estimates in Q4
by Zacks Equity Research

Utility stocks are expected to gain from new rates and expense management despite increase in interest rates.

Top Stocks To Beat Earnings

Symbol	ESP	Most Acc Est	Cons Est	ZRank
ADBE	0.14	1.61	1.61	3
TLRY	27.59	-0.11	-0.15	3
TCEHY	3.57	0.29	0.28	3

Earnings Analysis »

Are We Heading into an Earnings...
Earnings Outlook
by Sheraz Mian

While growth is no doubt decelerating, it is still positive and in-line with where are in economic cycle.

• Previewing Department Store Stock Earnings

Earnings Headlines

• American Public Education's (APEI) Q4...
• American Vanguard (AVD) Q4 Earnings Top,...
• York Water's (YORW) Q4 Earnings Beat...
• Inovio (INO) Misses on Q4 Earnings &...

Trending Top

Latest | Most Po|

New Strong Buys 1
4 Stocks to Profit h
AWS 3/13 Durabl
PFP 3/13 Stocks
Top Stock Picks f
6 Dividend ETFs

BLUEPRI INCOME

ZACKS CALENDAR OF EARNINGS

Zacks calendar of earnings shows is one page report. The report shows a trading week of an earnings release month, stock number that is expected to have earnings release. By clicking onto a trading day of the month, it shows the entire stock (company) list for earnings release on a trading day of the week. To move the presentation page forward at the page bottom click onto next and to move presentation backward click on previous.

EXHIBIT 13 – 6

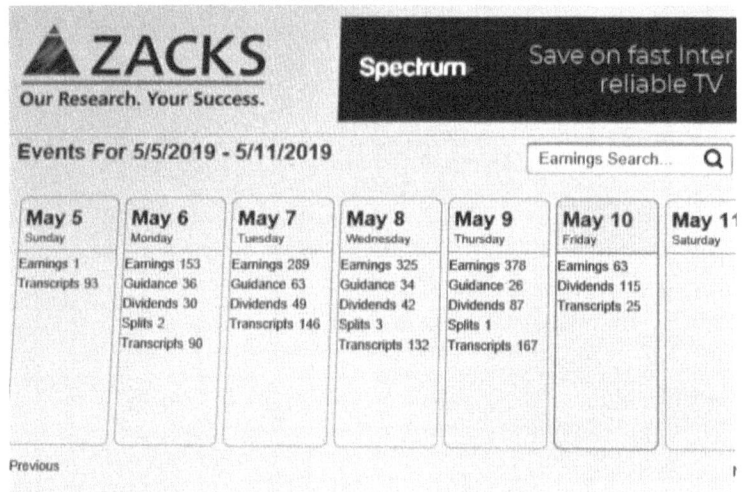

May 8, 2019 Earnings Announcements

		Earnings	Sales	Guidance	Revisions	Dividends	Splits	Transcripts				

Symbol	Company	Market Cap(M)	Time	Estimate	Reported	Surprise	%Surp	Price Change	Repo
ROKU	Roku, Inc.	7,142	amc	-0.24	-0.09	+0.15	+62.50%	28.11%	
DIS	The Walt Disney	201,240	amc	1.59	1.61	+0.02	+1.26%	-1.04%	
HEAR	Turtle Beach Co.	158	amc	0.03	0.13	+0.10	+333.33%	-1.76%	
CHK	Chesapeake Ener..	4,716	bmo	0.15	0.14	-0.01	-6.67%	3.96%	
CTL	Centurylink, In..	12,464	amc	0.27	0.34	+0.07	+25.93%	-4.99%	
ET	Energy Transfer..	39,500	amc	0.36	0.37	+0.01	+2.78%	-1.33%	

From Zacks Investment Research

GOOGL/NASDAQ/ZACKS EARNINGS FORECAST

GOOGL/NASDAQ/ZACK's is the next stock research source that has two pages. On the chrome or internet browser page you enter the statement stock symbol next earnings report date. The first page shows the requested stock symbol, earnings release date and if available it states the stock trading day earnings release time. To access a stock earnings forecast, on the page is a statement 'stock report date NASDAQ that you click onto. The second page states the analyst number who developed the stock forecast, the analyst earnings per share (EPS) as dollars forecast for the quarter and shows a stock EPS $ for the same quarter last year. The stock earnings per share ranking are indicated on a banner with red (sell), yellow or green (buy).

EXHIBIT 13 – 7
GOOGL/NASDAQ/ZACKS EARNINGS FORECAST

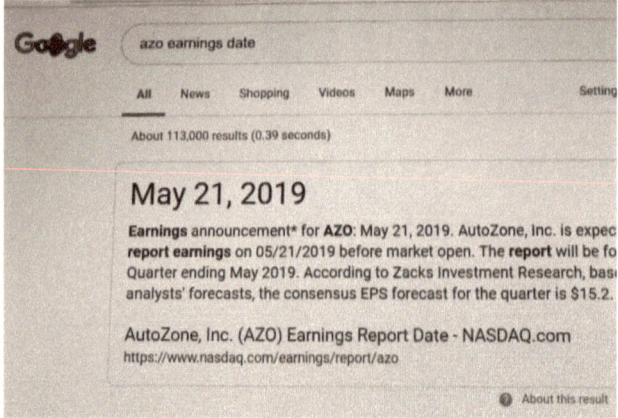

GOOGL/NASDAQ/ZACKS EARNINGS FORECAST CONTINUED

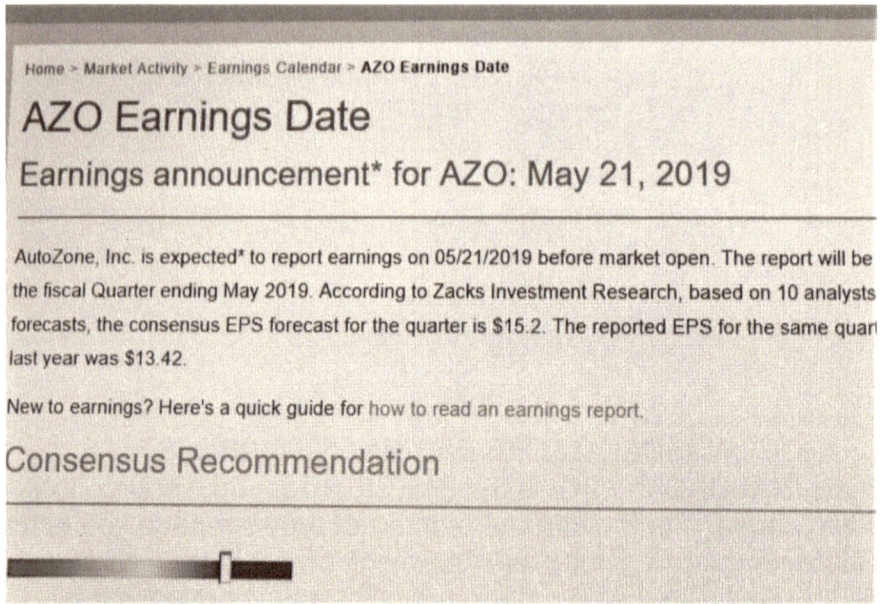

From GOOGL/NASDAQ/ZACK

EXHIBIT 13 – 8

BROKER STOCK RESEARCH

BROKER STOCK RESEARCH

Your Broker account (our example is Charles Schwab) stock research page is a one page report as a stock research resource. After you access your broker account, click onto account market position and then click onto a stock symbol. This click shows a broker stock research page for a stock that you clicked onto in your portfolio. If your interest is in a different stock research report, there is a rectangle on the page right side for you to enter your selected stock symbol. The page provides your requested stock symbol, recent market price, financial data, a stock price movement chart for your selected month period, states earnings release month and day of month, if available earnings release time of trading day and financial analyst numerical ranking by estimated earnings per share dollar value with high dollar estimate and low dollar estimate and stock last quarter estimate.

Also, the movement stock price movement chart shows the stock price history before an earnings release date and after an earnings release date. These figures help you to determine your stock purchase day number before a stock earning release date.

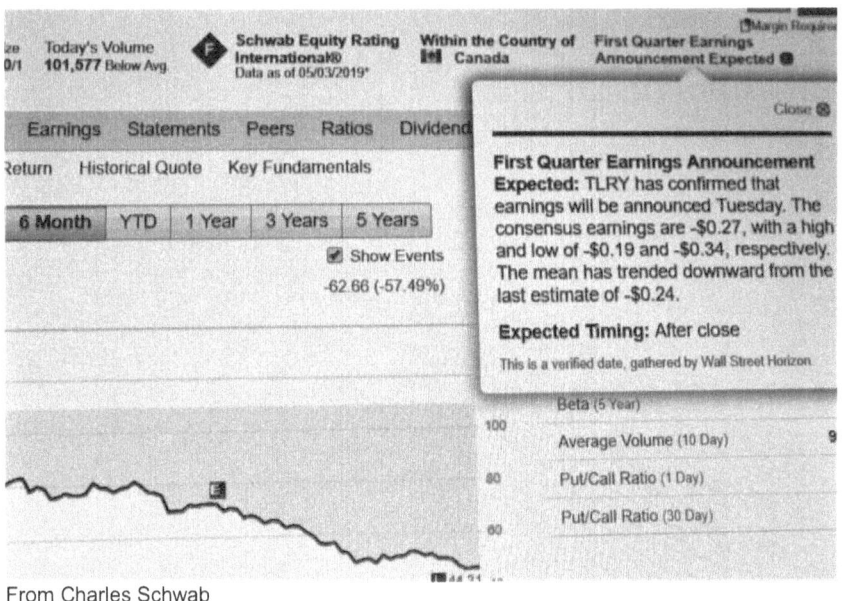

From Charles Schwab

CELL PHONE
Your cell phone with a broker program app and streaming CNBC TV app provides you with your broker trading access, stock price

information and portfolio information and real time stock market news, stock recent prices and ticker tape.

Cell phone app trading program is your broker program that is entered onto your cell phone. During regular trading hours, the app allows you to complete trade transactions through your broker program away from your computer (home) or get stock market stock price updates and other stock market information.

EXHIBIT 13 – 10

CELL PHONE BROKER TRADING PROGRAM

From Charles Schwab

A second Cell phone app, is an app for access to streaming CNBC TV program that provides real time and extended trading hours update for stock market and stock prices on the ticker tape and Extended hours stock earnings release.

EXHIBIT 13 – 11

CELL PHONE CNBC TV PROGRAM & TICKER TAPE

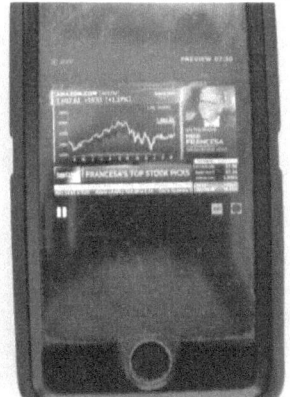

From CNBC TV

YAHOO

After you go on the interest net browser or chrome, for your next stock research source you go to Yahoo finance. The Yahoo finance page has a series of articles or news briefs that discuss a stock anticipated earnings release date, earnings release results, stock news, geo-political events, recent price, and other stock financial data.

EXHIBIT 13 – 12

YAHOO FINANCE NEWS

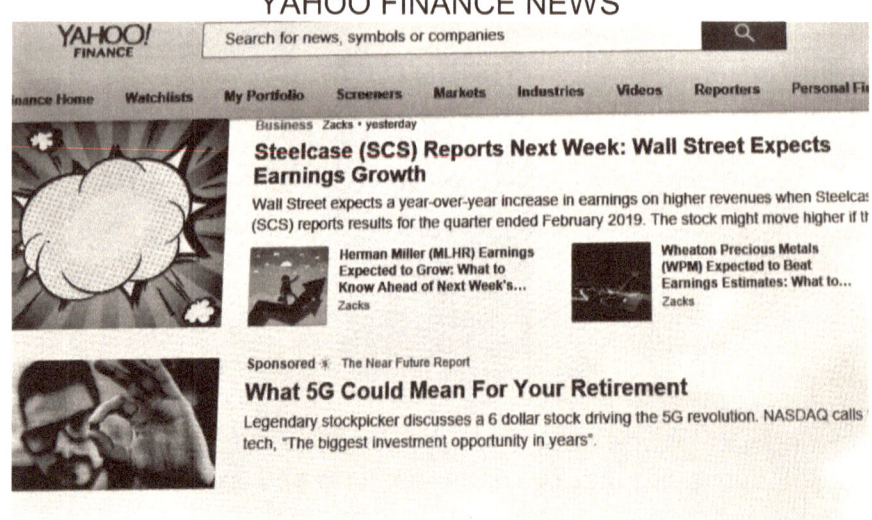

From Yahoo

YAHOO NEWS PAGE CONTINUED

From Yahoo

YAHOO calendar of earnings shows is one page report. The report shows a trading week of an earnings release month, stock number that is expected to have earnings release. By clicking onto a trading day of the month, it shows the entire stock

(company) list for earnings release on a trading day of the week. To move the presentation page forward at the page bottom click onto next and to move presentation backward
click on previous.

EXHIBIT 13 – 13
YAHOO STOCK EARNINGS CALENDAR

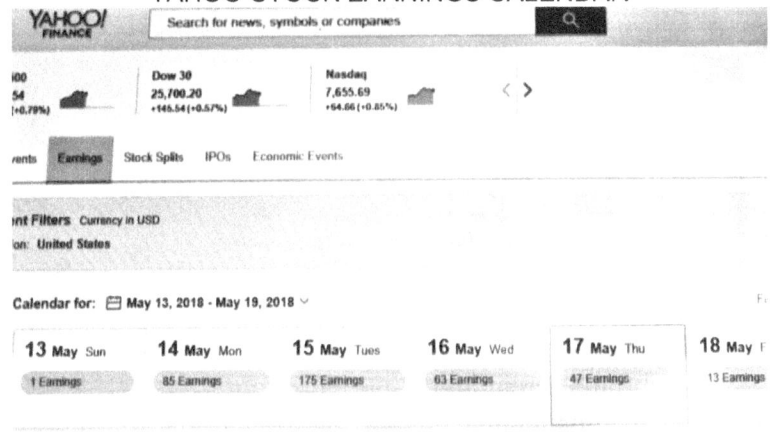

From Yahoo

YAHOO STOCK EARNINGS CALENDAR (Continued)

From Yahoo

BLOOMBERG CALENDAR OF EARNINGS

Bloomberg earnings calendar page is the next stock research source. For United States stocks you click on to United States and enter your selected trading day for earnings date. The sheet shows you the selected trading day stocks with expected earnings release.

EXHIBIT 13 – 14

BLOOMBERG CALENDAR OF EARNINGS

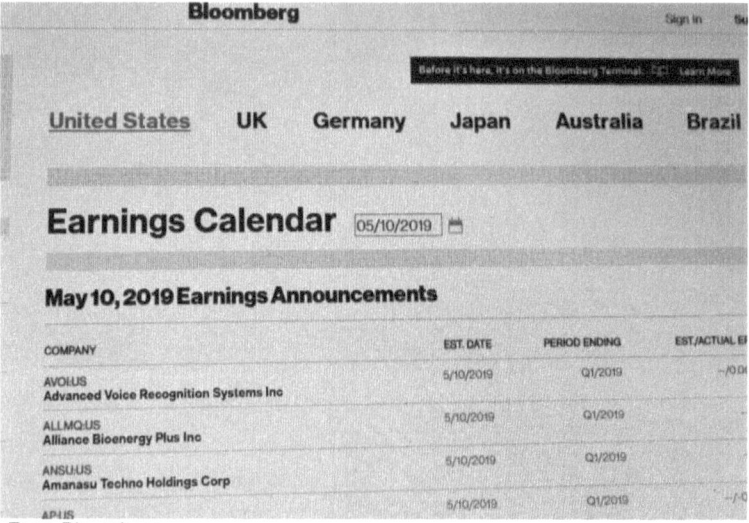

From Bloomberg

CHAPTER 14

CONSLUSION

In conclusion, the book 'Stock Investing Game Plan Sell After Earnings Report' A Stock Trading method has provided you with the insights, ability and desire to use Stock Investing Game Plan Sell After Earnings Report as you stock investment strategy.

A Stock Investing Game Plan Sell After Earnings Report a stock trading method features and advantages are

- With your on-line computer or cell phone app you can complete common stock trade transactions at home or anywhere
- Minimum Stock Investing Game Plan Sell After Earnings Report a stock trading method training that can be accomplished with paper trading
- With the Stock Investing Game Plan Sell After Earnings Report a stock trading method on your computer program, the Work Sheet & Spread Sheet
- Allows you with a recent stock market price to visualize your potential stock trade flat dollar ($) or (%) percent profit before you give your stock trade to your broker
- No additional investment programs required
- No common stock analysis experience required but willingness to complete stock research & market tracking
- Become financial independent
- Add to your retirement income
- Make money ($), enjoy life & add to your retirement income
- Increase your wealth for you & your family live comfortable
- Grow you money ($) sum
- Easy to acquire Stock Investing Game Plan Sell After Earnings Report a stock trading method skills
- If power goes down at your house and with a cell phone app and paper printed Stock Investing Game Plan Sell After Earnings a stock Report trading method Work Sheets and Computer Spread Screen Sheet you complete stock trades
- Teach your family members or friends or create a Stock Investing Game Plan Sell After Earnings Report a stock trading method club.

CHAPTER 15

GLOSSARY OF TERMS

Glossary Of terms are word that are associated with the Stock Investing Game Plan Sell After Earnings Report a stock trading method and as required monthly dividend common stock investment strategy. Each term's definition is written so you easily understand the book terms. Also, book terms provides you with common stock investment terms and knowledge that allows you to read and understand stock market articles or have stock market conversation with friends.

EPS   Earning per share is a corporation sale (total earnings in dollars) per common stock shares that are outstanding. To calculate earnings per share, corporation sales (total earnings) are divided by the number of outstanding common stock shares that are report on a corporation balance sheet. The EPS dollar value is a very important EPS date common stock trading component.

EPS =   corporation sales (total earnings)
          number of shares from a corporation balance sheet

ER Date   ER date is a quarterly calendar date that a corporation reports its sales (total earnings) as earnings per share. The ER date is a very important ER date common stock trading component.

Earnings Calendar a financial or stock broker company quarterly report lists expected dates for corporations to state their earnings per share. Some reports are a series of calendar dates. For each date, it lists corporations that are expected to have Earnings release, EPS common stock trading time to release earnings (Before Open, During Regular Hours or After Close), financial analyst ER value ranking and other important financial information. An Earnings Calendar Report is a very important research tool for ER date common stock trading activity.

Earnings Release Before Open has a corporation release ER earnings before the common stock market opens which is 900 PM. If you have extended hours trading feature with your stock broker, then you can trade before a common stock market open. With a corporation ER release and a ER positive release creates a common stock price increase that satisfies your profit objective, then before market open feature at 700 AM ET, you can complete common stock trade transactions (place sell or purchase orders) from 805 to 925 or during common stock market regular trading hours. For you to have maximum common stock trading flexibility, the Before Market feature or your broker extended hour trading feature is a very important EPS date common stock trading component.

Earnings Release During Trading Hours has a corporation release an Earnings during common stock market regular hours from 900 PM to 400PM. With regular stock common trading hours feature from your stock broker, then you can only trade common stocks within the regular stock market hour's time frame. During these hours a corporation Earnings release and Earnings release can have a common stock price increase that satisfies your profit objective, then your common stock trade (sell or purchase) options are within today's market regular house or during tomorrow market regular trading hours.

Earnings Release After Close has a corporation release it earnings after the common stock market closes which is 400 PM. If you have extended hours trading feature from your stock broker, then an after close market corporation EPS earnings release and earnings release can have a common stock price increase that satisfies your profit objective, then you complete a common stock transaction (sell or purchase orders) are after close common stock market from 405
to 800 PM ET or during tomorrow market regular common stock trading hours. For you to have maximum flexibility, After Close Market feature and your broker extended hour trading feature is a very important ER date common stock trading component.

Common Stock Market After a corporation completes a common stock Initial Public Offering (IPO), a corporation's common stock is traded in secondary markets that consist usually of the New York or NASDQA stock exchanges. These two exchanges together have the largest common stock share traded volume.

Initial Public Common Stock Offering An IPO has a private owned corporation contract with the stock broker firms to make a corporation common stock available to stock broker selected individuals (public) for purchase and the corporation becomes a publicly held common stock corporation and the corporation common stock is traded on the common stock market.

Common Stock is corporation share that entitles a share holder to a dividend payment as declared by a corporation board of directors and there is usually one veto per common share on a corporation issue

Common Stock Portfolio is an investor list of the various corporations' common stock shares owned and each associated common stock market value

Penny Common Stock is defined by SEC as a common stock that traders below $5 per common share

Preferred Stock is corporation share that entitles a shareholder to a fixed dividend payment amount and dividend payment is made before dividend payment to common shareholders. With most preferred stocks there are no voting rights

Stock Broker is an individual or corporation that has a seat a stock exchange where you common stock is listed and for a commission to complete your submitted purchase and sell common stock transactions. Also, a stock broker can control your buy and hold stock broker account

Stock Broker Cash Account is your account with a stock broker that requires you to have cash in the account and with cash in your account to complete all common stock purchase and sell transactions

Stock Broker Margin Account is an account with a stock broker firm that allows you to purchase common stock on borrowed bases as a percentage of your stock account common stock market value. Your amount to be borrowed on margin is controlled by stock broker and SEC established limits

To Trade Cash Settled Funds with a margin stock broker account all settled cash funds are the cash money that is available to an investor to write a check.

To Trade Available To Day Trade or Day Buying Power Funds with a margin stock broker account are a day trading money (cash or borrowed from stock broker) to complete common stock purchase transactions.

Cash & Borrowing Funds with a margin stock broker account is the cash or margin money available for marginable common stock purchase transactions.

Marginable Common Stock with a margin stock broker account is a common stock that your stock broker account will allow you to complete a margin purchase transaction.

Non-Marginable Common Stock with a margin stock broker account is a common stock that your stock broker account will not allow you to complete a normal margin purchase transaction but will restrict your common stock purchase (bit-coin common stocks) or will require additional reserve money as collateral such as 50% with marijuana stocks.

Stock Broker Regular Hours Trading Account is a stock broker account that allows you to complete common stock purchase and sell transactions between 900 and 400

Stock Broker Extended Hours Trading Account is a stock broker account that allows an investor to complete common stock transactions before the market opens (from 705 to 925) and after the stock market closes from 405 to 800

Stock Broker Commission is a stock broker dollar flat fee plus contract value that is placed on your common stock purchase transaction. The fee varies per stock broker corporation

Stock Exchange Sell Transaction Fee is a stock exchange dollar value that is a percentage that is charge for each common stock sell transaction

Analyst Estimate is a person or financial corporation professional who has an economic, financial, accounting degree or stock market working experience to mathematically and analytically project a common stock future price

Corporation Common Stock Guidance is an individual or corporation management sales/earnings forecast as to what they expect corporate sells to be in the future and the impact from industry and government policies on its business and sales. Poor corporate guidance usually decreases a common stock market price and is not preferred for ER
Date trading. Good, strong or growth corporate guidance increases a common stock market price and is preferred for ER stock trading

ER Date Trading ER Date trading is common stock investing strategy that has you create a qualified common stock list that is based on common stock analyst estimated report earnings release date and trading day report time and analyst ER rankings. You complete common stock research to determine the best qualified common stocks for a specific common stock trading date. 3 to 4 trading days prior to a common stock ER date, you complete common stock purchase transaction. A common stock purchase price with commission and exchange fees added to your common stock purchase price. On your work sheet and ER Date trading chart, a common stock price dollar value is listed adjacent to a common stock symbol, earnings date and ranking. After a common stock reports its earnings on the ER date with a positive earnings report, positive ER and strong corporation guidance, a common stock price increases and you sell a common stock at a profit.

Earnings Review is a corporation's earnings report that shows its past quarter earnings/sales as a beat or miss an analyst estimate. Earnings beat is preferred ER date common stock trading due to sell common stock at a profit. Earnings mess is not preferred for EPS date common stock trading due to you sell common stock at a loss

EPS earnings date is the quarterly calendar date that a corporation releases corporate sales/earnings

Earnings Calendar is a financial or stock broker corporation report. The report that lists a corporation expected to release quarterly earnings. Earnings calendar is a very important ER Date common stock trading research tool to develop a qualified common stock list for ER Date common stock trading method. In our ER Date trading method
practice we use at least two financial company or stock broker earnings calendars

Earnings Report Trading Day Time is the time of a common stock trading day that a corporation releases it earnings report. The various corporation earning report common stock trading day release times are Before Market Opens before 930, During Regular common stock
trading hours 930 to 400 and After Market Closes at 400

Bear Market Bull Market is a common stock bull market that usually has the majority or all common share market prices decreasing. For ER Date trading method a bear market is not preferred due to you sell common stocks at a loss

Bull Market is a common stock market that usually has the majority or all common share market prices rising. For ER Date trading method a bull market is preferred due to you sell common stocks at a profit

Stock Buy Back is a corporation established financial program (budget amount) to purchase common shares at the common stock market price from the common stock market. Usually a common stock buyback program reduces the number of common shares outstanding and improves future earnings per share

Stock Split Up or Reverse Split A common stock split up has corporation issues new corporate shares in proportion to a shareholder existing share this feature increases common stock shares outstanding. A reverse split has a corporation deceases the number of share and usually signals a corporation problem.

Paper Trading common stocks is a common stock trading training strategy that has you as a potential investor complete all common stock purchase and sell transactions on paper with no money changing hands.   Paper trading common stocks allows you to become familiar on how to navigate common stock purchase and sell transactions, obtain a positive experience and become motivated
to proceed to become an actual money common stock trader

Buy & Hold is a common stock market investing method that has you purchase and hold common stocks for a long time period (usually more than one year) and you do not sell common stock from your common stock portfolio as a common stock market price fluctuates.

Day Trading is common stock investing method that has you complete one or several stock purchase and sell transactions with one trading day. Example is on one trading day an investor purchases ABC stock in the morning and later in the afternoon sell ABC stock

Pattern Trading is common stock investing method that has you complete one or several stock purchase and sell transactions over a period of several common stock trading days. Example is an investor purchases ABC common stock in the Monday and later in the week on Thursday sell ABC common stock

Bid Price is a listed common stock market price that a purchaser is willing to pay or purchase a common stock

Ask Price is a listed common stock market price that a seller is willing to sell a common stock

Market Price is a trading day last common stock price for a purchase or sell transaction completion

Limit Price is a common stock market price to complete a purchase or sell transaction. With a limit common stock purchase price your common stock purchase transaction is completed at a common stock price that is as stated or below your limit common stock price. With a limit sell common stock price your common stock purchase transaction is completed at a common stock price that is as stated or above.

SEC is a US government agency to protect common stock investors by managing an efficient, transparent and effective common stock market

SECURITIES & EXCHANGE COMMISSION See SEC

NEW YORK STOCK EXCHANGE is largest common stock exchange in the USA per stock trade volume and common stocks listed

NASDAQ STOCK EXCHANGE is the second largest common stock exchange in the USA

Broker Assisted   Broker assisted common stock trading transaction has you direct a stock broker to complete your common stock purchase & sell transactions. Brokers charge a higher commission to complete a common stock transaction and all common stock transaction values are updated onto your portfolio market value

On-Line Computer Or Cell Phone App On-line computer or cell phone app common stock trading (purchase and sell) transaction is a broker account type that occurs over the internet from you to your stock broker account. All common stock transaction values are updated onto your portfolio market value. When compared to a broker assisted common stock transaction, on-line computer or cell phone app has a lower stock broker commission to complete a common stock transaction.

Halt Trading Halt trading is a SEC temporary common stock stop (halt) trading for a short time period (usually 1 to 2 hours) one or all exchanges. A halt trading is issued due to a corporation has notified the SEC that corporate news is to be released that could greatly impact a corporation's common stock market price.

Common Stock Investing Goal is your (investment) common stock trading financial objectives or expectations. Your common stock investment goals are based on your common stocking trading results direct you to have a profit. Your common stock investment goals are (1) expected flat dollar ($) increase or value to sell at a profit, (2) excepted percentage (%) increase on your investment to sell at a
profit , (3) unexpected common stock price decrease and you sell at the best possible price.

.

Bio-Sketch

David Mulcahy has been a self directed stock market investor for over \30 years. His first stock market investing method was an individual buy and hold stock investing method. Later a change in the stock market investment method was directed to dividend paying stocks investing method. The next stock investment strategy was monthly dividend paying stock method that created a monthly cash flow. These stock market investment methods, required to master stock market investing steps through a broker account. To achieve a higher income flow, he started the stock investing game plan sell after earnings report a stock investing method. The stock investing game plan sell after earnings report a stock investing method required him to complete stock research to qualified stocks, purchase qualified stocks and after a corporation releases earnings report to sell stocks. When compared to other stock investing methods, stock investing game plan sell after earnings report a stock investing method increased the sell stock profits and monthly cash flow.

INDEX

www.ingramcontent.com/pod-product-compliance
Lightning Source LLC
Chambersburg PA
CBHW030643220526
45463CB00004B/1624